FIRED INTO FREEDOM

HOW GETTING LET GO HELPED ME UNLOCK MILLIONS IN GRANTS
+ A STEP-BY-STEP GUIDE TO SECURING
$50K–$100K IN GRANTS
(EVEN IF YOU STILL HAVE A 9–5)

BY JEKWENTA "COACH K" PRIMM
– THE GRANT EXPERT™

DISCLAIMER

The advice contained in this material might not be suitable for everyone. The author designed the information to present her opinion about the subject matter. The reader must carefully investigate all aspects of any business decision before committing to him or herself. The author obtained the information contained herein from sources she believes to be reliable and from her own personal experience, but she neither implies nor intends any guarantee of accuracy. The author is not in the business of giving legal, accounting, or any other type of professional advice. Should the reader need such advice, he or she must seek services from a competent professional. The author particularly disclaims any liability, loss, or risk taken by individuals who directly or indirectly act on the information contained herein. The author believes the advice presented here is sound, but readers cannot hold her responsible for either the actions they take, or the risk taken by individuals who directly or indirectly act on the information contained herein.

Published by 1BrickPublishing

Printed in the United States

Copyright © 2025 by Jekwenta Primm

ISBN 979-8898560034

DEDICATION

To my daughter—my reason for everything. Thank you for being patient during those late nights at the daycare, for understanding when mommy had to "figure it out," and for showing me that true success means being present for what matters most.

To my parents who taught me the value of hard work, even if we took different paths.

And to every entrepreneur who's been told "no" by traditional funding sources but refused to give up on their dreams—this book is your roadmap to the "yes" you deserve.

Remember: Getting fired might just be your freedom ticket.

—Coach K

DEDICATION REQUEST

Please share this book with anyone who is struggling to fund their dreams or believes the doors of opportunity are closed to them. Share it with those who need to know that their vision deserves investment and that grants—the most overlooked funding source—could be their path to financial freedom.

TABLE OF CONTENTS

THE UNEXPECTED PATH TO MILLIONS

I never planned to get fired.

But there I was, sitting at my kitchen table on a Tuesday morning, staring at my laptop screen. The Zoom meeting request from my manager had come through earlier than our usual morning call. I already knew what was coming.

"Jekwenta, we need to discuss your outside business activities..."

After fifteen years at Wells Fargo, climbing the ranks, breaking sales records at branches others had written off, and bringing in million-dollar clients, my corporate journey was about to end. Not with the gold watch and retirement party I once imagined, but with a digital pink slip and a severance package that wouldn't last long.

My stomach knotted as I thought about my mortgage, my struggling childcare business, my daughter depending on me, and the mountain of bills piling up. To make matters worse, I was dealing with legal complications from a relationship gone wrong. It felt like everything was crashing down at once.

What I didn't know then was that this moment—this painful, terrifying moment of professional rejection—would become the catalyst for the most profound transformation of my life.

That termination call would eventually lead me to discover a largely untapped reservoir of funding that would not only save my business but launch me into an entirely new career helping others secure millions in grant money.

But I'm getting ahead of myself.

Hi, I'm Jekwenta Primm, but most people know me as Coach K, The Grant Expert™. I've helped entrepreneurs and small business owners secure over $5 million in grant funding. I've taught thousands of people how to find, apply for, and win grants they never knew existed or thought they could qualify for.

But before all that, I was just a corporate banker trying to juggle a side business, single motherhood, and the constant pressure to hit aggressive sales targets.

This book is the story of how getting fired became the best thing that ever happened to me—and how it can change your life too.

If you picked up this book, chances are you're in one of a few situations:

- Maybe you're struggling to keep your business afloat and desperately need funding that doesn't involve taking on more debt.
- Perhaps you're working a 9-to-5 that drains your energy while your entrepreneurial dreams sit on the back burner.
- Or you might be doing okay but know you're capable of so much more if you just had the capital to take the next step.

Wherever you are on your journey, I wrote this book for you.

In these pages, I'm going to share exactly how I went from broke and desperate to building a thriving business helping others access grant funding. I'm going to walk you through the step-by-step process I've developed for finding and winning grants—the same process that has helped my clients secure funding ranging from $500 to over $2.6 million.

But this isn't just a how-to manual. It's also a mindset revolution.

Because here's the truth: the biggest obstacle between you and funding isn't your business model, your background, or your credentials. It's how you think about money, support, and your own potential.

From Daddy's Girl to Determined Entrepreneur

To understand how I got here, you need to know where I started.

I was a spoiled rotten daddy's girl growing up in Tennessee. Anything I wanted was practically at my fingertips. Both my parents worked incredibly hard. My mom held the same job for 35 years, rarely missing a day of work. My dad was the only Black manager at his company and ran a side business remodeling homes.

They drilled into me the importance of education, hard work, and climbing the corporate ladder. The entrepreneurial spirit was there in my father's example, but it wasn't something they actively encouraged. The message was clear: get a good education, find a stable career, and work your way up.

I took that advice to heart. I went to college with dreams of becoming a sports and entertainment lawyer. I was on track until life threw me a curveball. During my senior year, I found out I was pregnant with my daughter.

Law school suddenly seemed impractical. I needed income now. So when a former colleague offered me a position at Wells Fargo, I jumped at the opportunity.

What began as a financial necessity turned into a fifteen-year career. I was good at banking—really good. I could walk into a branch that had never met its sales goals and turn it around within months. I built relationships with clients that brought millions in investments. I played the corporate game and played it well.

But something always felt off.

I remember the day my regional VP handed me an envelope after I closed a million-dollar loan—a deal I had sourced, qualified, and processed entirely on my own. Inside wasn't a bonus check or even a gift card. It was a certificate to order a Wells Fargo t-shirt from the company store.

A t-shirt. For bringing in over a million dollars.

That moment planted a seed of discontent that would grow over the years. But like many of you reading this, I stayed anyway. The steady paycheck, the benefits, the illusion of security—they were hard to walk away from, especially with a child depending on me.

The Side Hustle That Changed Everything

While working at Wells Fargo, I started a childcare center. My daughter needed quality care with extended hours, and I saw a business opportunity in solving this problem for other working parents.

Running a daycare while maintaining my banking career was exhausting. I'd work at the bank all day, then head to the childcare center until closing. My daughter and I would get home around 8 or 9 PM, leave just enough time for homework, dinner, and bed before starting all over again.

One evening, my daughter dropped a truth bomb that hit me hard. When I told her that one day the daycare could be hers, she replied, "I don't want to work at a daycare. It takes up all your time."

Talk about a wake-up call. The business I started to create more freedom was actually making me less present for the person who mattered most.

Meanwhile, Wells Fargo had started investigating my "outside business activities." They monitored my social media, interrogated me about my finances, and eventually gave me an ultimatum: dissolve my LLC or face termination.

The message was clear: you can be an employee or an entrepreneur, but not both.

I refused to shut down my business. So when that termination call finally came, it wasn't entirely unexpected. But that didn't make it any less terrifying.

Rock Bottom and The Grant Revelation

After getting fired, I faced the harsh reality of my financial situation. My childcare business was struggling due to changing regulations and requirements. Bills were piling up. I had maxed out my credit cards. I even applied for a loan from Wells Fargo while I still worked there and was declined.

I was at rock bottom, contemplating closing the daycare—the very business I had sacrificed so much to build.

That's when I remembered something. An older lady who helped with my daycare certifications had mentioned grants. "Girl, you need to apply for grants," she'd say. And every time, I'd dismiss her. "I ain't got time for that," I'd reply, assuming grants were only for nonprofits or required special training to apply for.

But desperate times call for desperate measures. With nothing to lose, I started researching grants.

I found a foundation offering small business grants and applied. The application took me less than 30 minutes to complete. A few weeks later, I received an approval letter for $500.

It wasn't a life-changing amount, but a lightbulb went off in my head.

Wait a minute. All I had to do was tell these people what I wanted to do with the money, spend 30 minutes filling out an application, and they gave me $500? I could do this all day long!

I began applying for more grants, learning the system, understanding what funders were looking for, and refining my approach. Soon, I was securing larger amounts. As I shared my success on social media, people started asking how they could do the same.

What began as a personal survival strategy evolved into coaching others. I held free workshops in Nashville and Huntsville that were packed wall to wall. People started calling me "Coach K," and the name stuck.

Over time, I developed a systematic approach to finding and winning grants—an approach that has now helped my clients secure millions in funding.

The Truth About Grants

Before we go any further, let's address some myths that might be holding you back from pursuing grant funding:

Myth #1: You have to be a nonprofit to qualify for grants.

This is perhaps the biggest misconception out there. While it's true that many grants are designated for nonprofit organizations, there are thousands of grants specifically for for-profit businesses. You just need to know where to look and how to position yourself.

Myth #2: You need to hire a grant writer or be certified in grant writing.

Grant writers typically charge between $5,000 and $10,000 with no guarantee of success. Why pay someone else when you can learn to do it yourself? Grant applications aren't as complicated as you might think. With the right guidance, anyone can write a winning application.

Myth #3: Grants are just free money for struggling businesses.

Funders aren't looking to bail out failing businesses. They're looking to invest in people and ideas that align with their mission and can deliver results. Grants aren't charity—they're strategic investments in solutions to problems funders care about.

Myth #4: The competition is too fierce; I'll never win.

Yes, grants are competitive. But most people never even apply because they believe these myths or don't know where to start. By simply submitting a well-crafted application, you're already ahead of the majority who never try.

The truth is, grants are an underutilized funding source that can transform your business without the burden of debt. They're not just for the elite, the well-connected, or those with fancy degrees. They're for anyone willing to learn the system and put in the work.

And that's exactly what I'm going to teach you in this book.

What You'll Learn

This book is divided into four parts, each designed to take you on a journey from wherever you are now to grant funding success.

Part I: The Journey shares my story in more detail—not because I love talking about myself, but because I want you to see that success doesn't happen overnight or in a straight line. My journey was messy, filled with setbacks, doubts, and difficult choices. I share it transparently so you can find parallels to your own experience and draw strength from knowing that your challenges can become stepping stones rather than roadblocks.

Part II: The Mindset dives into the psychological shifts that must happen before you can truly succeed with grants or any other funding. I'll talk about the independence trap—the belief that asking for help somehow diminishes your accomplishment. I'll show you how to find the right mentors and support system, and how to develop an abundance mindset that attracts opportunities rather than repels them.

Part III: The Grant Blueprint is where we get practical. I'll walk you through my proven process for finding and winning grants:

- How to structure your business for grant eligibility
- Essential documentation you need to have ready
- How to position your business to appeal to funders
- Where to find grants that match your business
- How to write compelling applications that stand out
- Common mistakes that get applications rejected
- What to do after you win (or don't win) a grant

This section includes real examples, templates, and scripts you can adapt for your own applications.

Part IV: Success Stories and Next Steps brings everything together with inspiring case studies of real people who have used my methods to secure funding. I'll also give you a 30-day action plan to kick-start your grant-seeking journey, complete with weekly goals and accountability measures.

By the end of this book, you'll have everything you need to go from idea to application to funding. But more importantly, you'll have the confidence and mindset to pursue grants as an ongoing funding strategy for your business.

Why Grants Matter More Than Ever

In today's economy, traditional funding paths are becoming increasingly difficult to navigate, especially for women and minority business owners.

Bank loans come with strict requirements and high interest rates. Venture capital is accessible to less than 1% of businesses, with women and minorities receiving a tiny fraction of those funds. Crowdfunding works for some but requires a significant following and marketing budget.

Grants offer a different path—one that doesn't require perfect credit, rich connections, or giving away equity in your business.

When I got that first $500 grant, I realized something profound: there are organizations with money that want to give it to people solving problems they care about.

The key is positioning your business not just as a profit-making entity but as a solution to a problem funders want to solve.

This shift in thinking—from "I need money to survive" to "I have a solution that deserves funding"—changes everything. It transforms you from a supplicant to a partner, from desperate to strategic.

And that's the greatest lesson I learned from my firing: when one door closes, you don't just look for another door—you build your own house.

Independence Doesn't Mean Isolation

One of the hardest lessons I had to learn was that independence doesn't mean doing everything alone.

Growing up as a daddy's girl, I always had the luxury of picking up the phone and getting whatever I needed. When I set out on my own, I was determined to make it without asking for help. I wanted to prove I could do it myself.

That mindset nearly ruined me.

When my business was struggling, when I was fired, when legal troubles hit—I still resisted reaching out. I saw asking for help as a sign of weakness rather than a strategic move toward strength.

It took hitting rock bottom for me to realize that the truly successful people aren't the ones who do everything alone. They're the ones who build strong support systems, who know when to ask for help, and who leverage resources available to them.

Grants taught me this lesson in a profound way. Applying for a grant isn't begging—it's proposing a partnership. You're not asking for charity; you're offering value. You're saying, "I have a solution to a problem you care about, and with your funding, I can implement it more effectively."

This mindset shift—from isolation to collaboration—changed everything for me. It opened doors I never knew existed and created opportunities I couldn't have imagined.

And it will do the same for you.

From Employee to Entrepreneur: The Real Transition

Many books talk about the practical aspects of transitioning from employee to entrepreneur—setting up your business, finding clients, managing your time. But few address the deeper identity shift that must occur.

When I worked at Wells Fargo, my identity was wrapped up in my job title, my team, my office. I knew exactly what was expected of me, when to show up, what success looked like.

Entrepreneurship stripped all that away. Suddenly, I had to define success for myself. I had to create structure rather than follow it. I had to lead rather than be led.

This transition is jarring for most people. It's why many return to employment even after starting promising businesses. The psychological comfort of defined roles and expectations is powerful.

But if you can push through this discomfort—if you can embrace the uncertainty and redefine your identity as the creator of your own path rather than a follower of someone else's—the rewards are beyond measure.

For me, those rewards included:

- Freedom to create a schedule that prioritizes my daughter
- The ability to help others access funding they never knew existed
- Financial independence that doesn't depend on a single employer
- The satisfaction of building something that reflects my values

- The joy of seeing clients transform their businesses with grant funding

These rewards didn't come immediately. There were months of struggle, doubt, and ramen noodle dinners. There were moments I considered sending out my resume and begging for another corporate job.

But I'm so glad I persisted. Because the life I have now—the impact I'm able to make, the freedom I enjoy, the legacy I'm building for my daughter—is worth every difficult moment along the way.

Your Grant Journey Starts Now

As you read this book, I want you to know that you already have everything you need to succeed with grants. You don't need special credentials, insider connections, or years of experience.

What you need is:

- A problem you're solving through your business
- A willingness to learn and adapt
- Persistence in the face of rejection
- A vision for what your funding will achieve

I had none of the traditional advantages when I started. I was a single mom with a failing business, mounting debt, and no safety net. What I had was determination and a willingness to try something new when the old ways weren't working.

That's all you need to start.

Throughout this book, I'll share stories of people just like you who have secured grants ranging from a few thousand dollars to over two million. People like Kathy, who had no background in grant writing but secured $40,000 within her first four months using my methods. Or Emma, who's received nearly a million dollars in funding. Or Megan, who's secured $2.6 million across three different organizations.

These aren't exceptional cases. They're regular people who followed a proven process and didn't give up when faced with obstacles.

You can do this too. And I'm going to show you exactly how.

How To Use This Book

To get the most from this book, I recommend reading it in order the first time through. My story provides context for the strategies, and the mindset shifts are necessary before you dive into the practical aspects.

Keep a notebook handy to jot down ideas specific to your business as you read. When you reach Part III: The Grant Blueprint, be prepared to do some work. The exercises and templates in this section are not just for show—they're the exact tools I use with my clients who have secured millions in funding.

Highlight sections that resonate with you, dog-ear pages you'll want to return to, and use the 30-day action plan in Part IV as your roadmap once you've finished reading.

Most importantly, commit to completing at least one grant application by the time you finish this book. Taking action, even imperfect action, is the only way to move forward.

The Fired Into Freedom Promise

I can't promise you'll win the first grant you apply for. I can't promise you'll secure millions in funding overnight. Anyone who makes such promises is selling you a fantasy.

What I can promise is this:

If you follow the process outlined in this book, you will find grants you qualify for. You will submit applications that have a realistic chance of approval. And you will develop a funding strategy that can sustain your business for years to come.

I can also promise that the skills you develop through this process—clear communication, strategic thinking, problem-solving, and persistence—will benefit every aspect of your business, whether you win grants or not.

But here's what I know from experience: grants are an underutilized funding source with less competition than you might think. Most business owners never even apply because they don't know where to start or believe they won't qualify.

By picking up this book, you've already separated yourself from the crowd. You've taken the first step toward a funding source that has transformed thousands of businesses, including my own.

My Why—And Yours

When I look back at my journey—from spoiled daddy's girl to corporate banker to fired and broke to grant expert—I see a path that makes perfect sense in retrospect but felt chaotic while I was living it.

The thread that ties it all together is financial education and empowerment.

It started when I worked at that payday loan company during college and saw a woman who had been paying $87.50 every two weeks for years without making a dent in her $500 loan. When I calculated how much she had paid over time and showed her, she broke down crying.

That moment lit a fire in me. I saw how lack of financial knowledge was trapping people in cycles of debt and dependence. I wanted to help but didn't know how.

Years later, when I discovered grants, I realized I had found my vehicle for change. Grants aren't just money—they're a paradigm shift. They represent a funding model based on value creation and problem-solving rather than extraction and interest payments.

My mission now is to become the "Earn Your Leisure of grants"—to democratize access to this funding source and change the narrative around who deserves capital and why.

So as you read this book, I encourage you to clarify your own "why." What problem are you solving? What impact will funding allow you to make? Who will benefit from your success beyond yourself?

These questions aren't just philosophical—they're practical. Your answers will form the foundation of your grant applications and determine which funding sources are the best match for your business.

Let's Get Started

Getting fired was the best thing that ever happened to me. It forced me to face challenges I was avoiding, discover resources I never knew existed, and build something far more valuable than the career I lost.

I don't know what brought you to this book. Maybe you're facing a crisis like I was. Maybe you're planning your exit from the 9-to-5 world. Maybe you're already running a business but need capital to grow.

Whatever your situation, I want you to know this: the path to funding is clearer than you think. The resources you need are more accessible than you've been led to believe. And your business—yes, yours—has value that deserves investment.

In the following pages, I'm going to show you exactly how to access those resources and communicate that value. I'm going to walk with you step by step through the process of finding, applying for, and winning grants.

All I ask is that you come with an open mind and a willingness to try something new. Because the funding landscape is changing, and those who adapt will thrive.

Are you ready to get fired into freedom?

Let's go.

—Jekwenta "Coach K" Primm The Grant Expert™

CHAPTER 1

FOUNDATIONS

"**A**lways showing up, going all in... even when you don't feel like it, you still show up and give it your all."

That was my mother's mantra. For 35 years, she worked for the same company, rarely missing a day. A woman who believed in the power of consistency, dedication, and the traditional path to success.

My daddy? He was a builder. Not just of homes—though he could "build and restructure anything"—but of dreams. He was the only Black manager at his company, a position he earned through relentless work and undeniable skill. And on the side, he ran his own home construction business, laying the foundation for what would become my first glimpse into entrepreneurship.

Spoiled rotten daddy's girl. That's how I'd describe my childhood self. Anything I wanted was at my fingertips. I didn't even pump my own gas until college—that's how much my daddy took care of me. But with that privilege came a front-row seat to what hard work looked like. Both my parents climbed into management roles. Both showed me what it meant to be excellent in whatever you do.

But they also showed me, unintentionally, the fragility of traditional employment.

I was young when it happened, but the memory is crystal clear. My father came home one day with news that would shift something in my understanding of the world. His company had gathered all the managers and asked them a simple question: "What would happen if you were terminated?"

One by one, they answered. When my father's turn came, he had a different response than the others. "I have my own business on the side," he said. "I'd be okay."

Shortly after, they let him go.

I didn't realize until much later, until my own firing actually, how significant that moment was. It was my first lesson in why corporate America often feels threatened by entrepreneurial employees. They want your loyalty, your complete dependence. The moment you demonstrate that you could survive without them, you become a threat.

My father went all in on his home construction company after that, doing real estate, rehabs, and remodeling. Eventually, he found his way back to traditional employment, but that seed was planted in me, even if I wouldn't nurture it until decades later.

My parents divorced when I was seven, but you wouldn't know it from how they co-parented. They showed up together for everything—my games, my school events, and later, my daughter's milestones. There was never separation in how they presented themselves as my parents. To this day, people are surprised to learn they weren't together all those years.

Growing up, I had big dreams. By sixth grade, I knew I wanted to be a lawyer. We had read a book in class and had to form debate teams based on it. Something clicked when I stood up and argued my point to victory. The feeling of articulating my thoughts, persuading others through reason and rhetoric—it lit me up inside.

"I might want to be a lawyer," I thought. And that dream stayed with me all the way through college.

Around the same time, I fell in love with sports. My grandmother insisted we watch the Tennessee Titans every Sunday at family dinner. They were new to Tennessee then, having just moved from being the Houston Oilers. Those Sundays planted a seed that would grow into a passion.

As I got older, I refined my dream: I wanted to be a sports or entertainment lawyer. I researched the field and discovered there weren't many Black women in this space. That only made me more determined. I didn't need to follow the typical path—I could go to law school and carve out my own niche.

But life, as it often does, had other plans.

The Misconceptions

One of the biggest misconceptions people had about me growing up was that everything was handed to me. Yes, I was spoiled in many ways, but there was so much more to my story.

My mother had my sister when she was just 15 years old. Growing up, I heard the whispers, the predictions: "You're going to be like your mom." "You'll get pregnant at 15 too." When my sister broke that so-called "generational curse" by not getting pregnant as a teen, the pressure and predictions shifted to me.

"Jekwenta's gonna do it. She's gonna get pregnant at 15."

But I didn't. And when that prediction failed, they adjusted: "Oh, when she goes off to college, she's gonna come back pregnant."

I didn't come back from college pregnant either. But I did get pregnant at the end of my senior year, right when my professional life was supposed to begin. Right when law school was on the horizon.

Those external expectations—both the ones that assumed I'd get everything handed to me and the ones that assumed I'd fail—fueled me with a fierce determination to prove people wrong. To show them I was more than their limited perception of me.

It's funny how others' doubts can become your greatest motivation. Every time someone said I couldn't or wouldn't, something in me sparked. "Watch me," that spark said. "Just watch what I can do."

The First Job

College was my first taste of independence. I deliberately chose to go away for school, to step out of the comfort zone of being daddy's girl and forge my own path. But that independence came with responsibilities.

During my sophomore year, I decided I wanted to move off campus. My parents had a simple rule: if I moved off campus, I needed to get a job. Fair enough.

So I walked into a place called Advance America, a payday loan company, and asked for an application. The manager interviewed me on the spot and hired me the same day. Lucky me, right?

What started as a part-time job to pay for my off-campus apartment quickly became much more. Despite being a student, I worked hard and eventually became a part-time assistant manager. I built relationships with our customers, many of whom became like family.

But I also witnessed something troubling.

Payday loans work like this: You come in and take out a loan based on your income. Let's say you make $700 every two weeks. They'll give you a $500 loan, but you have to come back and pay $587.50 when you get paid. The problem? If all you make is $700 every two weeks, how can you afford to lose $587.50 and still cover your expenses? You can't. So you take out the loan again. And again. And again.

I started noticing the same faces coming in, paying that $87.50 fee every two weeks, trapped in a cycle they couldn't escape. One day, curiosity got the better of me. I pulled out a customer's folder—a woman who had been coming in since the store opened in 1999. For years, she had been paying $87.50 every two weeks on that same $500 loan.

I got out a calculator and showed her: "This is how much you've given this company over the years." The number was staggering. She broke down crying right there in the store.

That was a pivotal moment for me. I saw with crystal clarity the devastating impact of financial illiteracy. My people—Black folks, working-class folks—were being trapped by predatory systems they didn't fully understand. And it wasn't because they weren't smart. It was because no one had ever taught them how money really works.

I decided then that I wanted to do something in finance, something that would educate and empower rather than extract and exploit.

Shortly after that realization, a former colleague who had left Advance America for Wells Fargo called me. "I want you to come work for me," he said. Initially, I declined. Banking wasn't in my plan—I was still thinking about law school.

But then I found out I was pregnant.

Suddenly, law school seemed like a distant dream. I needed stability, income, benefits—and I needed them now. My parents would have supported me, would have made sure my baby and I were okay while I went to law school. But something in me needed to stand on my own, to provide for my child myself.

So I accepted the position at Wells Fargo, purchased my first home, and stepped into a career that would span the next fifteen years of my life.

I loved it at first. The challenge of it, the relationships with clients, the satisfaction of helping people make smart financial decisions. At Wells Fargo, I found myself assigned to a branch downtown that had never met its sales goals. "You don't want to work there," people warned me. "It's a slow branch. People never meet their sales goals there."

But I've never been one to shy away from a challenge. In my interview, I told them, "I'll just make sure everybody on the street knows my name and what I do. They'll start sending me people." And that's exactly what happened.

I started meeting my sales goals consistently in a branch where that was supposedly impossible. I'd go out and find the business instead of waiting for it to come to me. I'd strike up conversations with anyone and everyone, uncovering opportunities others missed.

Like the time I met a gentleman who mentioned he was buying apartment complexes with partners from Michigan. I built a relationship with him, starting small with a savings account. Months later, he returned, ready to buy a million-dollar apartment complex. I connected him with the right opportunity, processed the deal, and closed on a loan worth over a million dollars.

My VP came to congratulate me. "Nobody's ever closed a million-dollar loan at this branch," he said, beaming with pride. Then he handed me an envelope.

Inside was a certificate to purchase a t-shirt from the company's website.

A t-shirt. For bringing in over a million dollars of business.

That moment stuck with me. It wasn't just the insulting nature of the reward. It was what it represented: a fundamental disconnect between the value I was creating and what the company was willing to give back. I had sourced the client, qualified him, closed the deal—and all I got was a t-shirt I couldn't even wear once I no longer worked there.

That was the first moment I thought, "Yeah, this isn't going to work for me."

But like many of you reading this book, I stayed anyway. The steady paycheck, the benefits, the illusion of security—these are powerful forces keeping us tethered to jobs that don't value us properly. And when you have a child depending on you, walking away feels even more impossible.

So I stayed. For many more years, I stayed. But that moment planted a seed of discontent that would eventually grow into something much larger—a desire for true independence, for building something of my own where the rewards matched the value I created.

I just didn't know yet what that something would be.

The Entrepreneurial Spark

While working at Wells Fargo, I decided to open a childcare center. My motivation was practical: I needed quality, affordable childcare with extended hours for my daughter. Looking around, I couldn't find options that met my needs, so I created one.

The daycare my daughter was attending was closing down, and I saw an opportunity. The director was amazing with the children but struggled with the business side. I thought we could partner—she would handle the childcare aspect, and I would manage the business operations.

I jumped in without really knowing what I was doing. I thought my background in finance meant I understood business. I didn't. There were so many aspects of running a childcare center I hadn't considered—licensing requirements, staff-to-child ratios, state funding regulations, curriculum development.

We opened with just two kids, including my daughter. But the state required a minimum number of employees to operate, so I had five staff members on payroll with barely any revenue coming in. Talk about pressure.

Fortunately, one of my coworkers gained custody of four children from a relative, and she brought them all to my daycare. Suddenly, we had nine kids and things were looking up. Word of mouth spread, especially among my Wells Fargo colleagues, and soon the center was doing well.

But then the regulations changed. The requirements for state funding shifted. The teacher-to-student ratio requirements were adjusted. What had been a thriving business began to struggle. My Wells Fargo paycheck was now keeping the daycare afloat rather than the other way around.

Balancing both roles was exhausting. I'd work at the bank all day, then head straight to the childcare center until closing. My daughter and I would get home around 8 or 9 PM, leaving just enough time for home-work, dinner, and bed before starting all over again.

One evening, my daughter, who was about 5 or 6 at the time, said some-thing that stopped me in my tracks. I had made a casual comment about passing the daycare down to her someday, and she replied, "I don't want to work at a daycare. It takes up all your time."

Out of the mouths of babes. The business I had started to create more freedom for us was actually making me less present. I had fallen into the same trap that catches so many entrepreneurs—working twice as hard for the promise of a freedom that never materializes.

Meanwhile, Wells Fargo had begun to take notice of my "outside business activities." It started innocently enough. They monitored social media and noticed posts about personal credit repair. When they questioned me, I explained it was my cousin's business and I had just shared her post.

But that was just the beginning. Soon they were asking about business credit and grants. They found my registered LLC for consulting services and began a full investigation. They went through my website, my social media accounts, even my business finances.

Eventually, they gave me an ultimatum: dissolve the LLC within 24 hours or face termination.

I refused. The message was clear: you can be an employee or an entrepreneur, but not both—at least not in their eyes.

So when that termination call finally came, it wasn't entirely unexpected. But that didn't make it any less terrifying.

The Foundation of It All

Looking back at my childhood, my education, my early career—all of it laid the foundation for where I am today.

My parents taught me the value of consistency, excellence, and hard work. My father showed me that entrepreneurship was possible, even if it wasn't explicitly encouraged. My mother demonstrated that showing up, day after day, was a form of power in itself.

My early fascination with debate and law developed my ability to articulate ideas clearly and persuasively—a skill that would prove invaluable when writing grant applications.

My time at Advance America opened my eyes to the devastating impact of financial illiteracy and predatory systems, igniting a passion for financial education that still drives me today.

My years at Wells Fargo taught me how to build relationships, identify opportunities, and deliver results—all while showing me exactly what I didn't want from my career.

And my experience starting a childcare center, with all its challenges and missteps, gave me a crash course in real-world business that no degree could provide.

Even the naysayers who predicted I'd follow a certain path served a purpose: they fueled my determination to prove them wrong, to chart my own course.

All of these experiences—the good, the bad, and the ugly—were preparing me for something I couldn't yet see. They were building the foundation for what would become my true calling: helping entrepreneurs access the funding they need to build their dreams without falling into debt traps.

I didn't know it then, but every challenge was a lesson. Every setback was preparation. Every moment was bringing me closer to my purpose.

And it would take getting fired—losing what I thought was my security—to finally find my way.

Your Foundation

As we close this chapter, I want you to think about your own foundation. What experiences have shaped you? What skills have you developed, perhaps without even realizing their value? What setbacks have taught you lessons that prepared you for something greater?

Often, we dismiss our backgrounds if they don't fit a certain mold. We think we need specific credentials or experiences to succeed. But your unique journey—with all its twists and turns—has equipped you with perspectives and abilities that no one else has.

Maybe you've been a stay-at-home parent, mastering the art of multitasking and negotiation. Perhaps you've worked in retail, developing keen insights into what motivates people to buy. Or you might have overcome personal challenges that gave you empathy and resilience others lack.

Whatever your path has been, it matters. It's part of what makes your business unique. And as you'll learn in later chapters, this uniqueness is precisely what can make your grant applications stand out.

Your background isn't a limitation—it's an asset. You just need to learn how to position it effectively.

In the next chapter, I'll take you deeper into my banking years and show you how the very career I thought was my security became the catalyst for my biggest transformation. We'll explore the warning signs I ignored, the skills I developed, and the mindset shifts that began during this period.

But for now, take a moment to appreciate your own foundation. Because everything you've experienced—everything you are—is preparing you for what's next.

And trust me, what's next is better than anything you've left behind.

CHAPTER 2

THE BANKING YEARS

"If you're making so much money with this daycare, why are you still working here?"

The investigator's question hung in the air like a challenge, but it wasn't the first red flag I should have noticed. By the time Wells Fargo called me into that conference room with their team of investigators, treating me like a criminal for having a second source of income, I had already been ignoring warning signs for years.

Let me take you back to those fifteen years at Wells Fargo—years that taught me everything about corporate America while slowly revealing why I could never truly belong there.

THE AGGRESSIVE SALES CULTURE

Wells Fargo had a reputation for aggressive sales goals, and if you've followed the news over the years, you know this wasn't exactly a secret. Employees were expected to hit monthly quotas that seemed to get more demanding every quarter. The pressure was so intense that some people would open unauthorized accounts just to meet their numbers.

I didn't go that route. Instead, I threw myself into the challenge with everything I had.

When I was assigned to that downtown branch—the one everyone said was a dead end—I saw it as an opportunity to prove myself. "I'll just make sure everybody on the street knows my name and what I do," I told them in my interview. "They'll start sending me people."

And that's exactly what I did.

I'd walk the streets during my lunch break, striking up conversations with business owners, shop employees, anyone who would talk to me. I'd attend networking events after work. I made it my business to become the go-to banking person in that area.

It worked. I started consistently hitting sales goals in a branch where that was supposedly impossible. Month after month, I exceeded expectations. I was building a reputation as someone who could turn around under-performing locations.

The work was satisfying in a way. There's something addictive about being excellent at your job, about being the person others look to when they need results. I loved the relationships I built with clients, the problem-solving aspect of banking, the feeling of helping people make smart financial decisions.

But beneath the surface, something was eating at me.

THE MILLION-DOLLAR WAKE-UP CALL

The moment that crystallized everything for me happened on what should have been one of my proudest days at Wells Fargo.

I had been out doing my usual street work—meeting potential clients, building relationships—when I struck up a conversation with a gentleman who mentioned he was in real estate. Not just any real estate—he was buying apartment complexes with partners from Michigan. These weren't small-time investors. We're talking about serious money.

I started small with him, as you do. He opened a savings account, testing me out. A few months later, he came back ready to make a major move. He wanted to purchase an apartment complex, and the deal was worth just over a million dollars.

I walked him through the entire process. I qualified him, connected him with the right loan officer, managed the paperwork, and saw the deal through to closing. This wasn't just about hitting my monthly quota—this was a major win for the bank.

When it was all finalized, my VP made a special trip from his office in another building to congratulate me. "This is huge," he said, beaming. "Nobody's ever closed a million-dollar loan at this branch."

The whole team was buzzing. They were shouting me out on company calls, sending congratulatory emails. For a moment, I felt like I was finally being recognized for the value I brought to the organization.

Then my VP handed me an envelope.

I opened it, expecting maybe a bonus check or at least a substantial gift card. Instead, I found a certificate that would allow me to order a t-shirt from the company's online store.

A t-shirt.

For bringing in over a million dollars of business.

I stood there holding that certificate, feeling something shift inside me. Not just disappointment—though I was certainly disappointed—but a profound realization about how this company valued my contributions.

I had sourced the client through my own networking. I had built the relationship from scratch. I had guided a complex deal from initial conversation to final closing. And my reward was a piece of clothing that I couldn't even wear outside of work without looking like a walking billboard for a company that clearly didn't value me.

"Yeah, this isn't going to work for me," I thought. But like so many of you reading this, I stayed anyway.

THE COMFORT TRAP

Why do we stay in situations that don't serve us? Why do we tolerate being undervalued when we know our worth?

The answer is complex, but it boils down to what I call the comfort trap. Even when we're unhappy, there's comfort in the familiar. There's security in a steady paycheck, benefits, a defined role with clear expectations.

For me, that comfort was amplified by having a daughter who depended on me. Walking away from a stable income felt irresponsible, even reckless. What if my business ideas didn't work out? What if I couldn't find another job? What if I was making a terrible mistake?

These fears kept me tethered to Wells Fargo even as my dissatisfaction grew. I told myself I was being practical, responsible, mature. Really, I was being scared.

The irony is that by staying in a situation where I was undervalued, I was teaching my daughter that accepting less than you're worth is normal. I was modeling the very mindset I desperately wanted her to avoid.

But I couldn't see that then. All I could see was the risk of leaving versus the safety of staying.

THE ENTREPRENEURIAL ITCH

Despite my hesitation to leave corporate banking, I couldn't shake the entrepreneurial itch. Maybe it was my father's influence, that early lesson about having multiple income streams. Maybe it was the financial literacy gap I'd witnessed at Advance America. Or maybe it was simply the natural evolution of someone who had always exceeded expectations in employee roles.

Whatever the source, I found myself drawn to the idea of building something of my own.

The childcare center was my first real foray into entrepreneurship, born out of a practical need for quality, affordable care for my daughter. As I mentioned in the previous chapter, the center was doing well for a while.

We had gone from two kids to nearly full capacity, and I was advertising heavily among my Wells Fargo network.

But what I didn't fully anticipate was how the bank would react to my success.

THE INVESTIGATION BEGINS

The first hint of trouble came in the form of a casual question about my Facebook activity. Someone from HR called to ask if I helped people with personal credit repair. I explained that I had shared a post from my cousin who did credit repair work.

"We're just making sure there's no conflict of interest," they said. Fair enough, I thought.

But the questions didn't stop there.

A few weeks later, they called again. "Do you help people with business credit and grants?" This time, I was hosting free webinars and speaking occasionally at events. I confirmed that yes, I did share information about business funding from time to time.

"Okay, we just wanted to check," they said.

Then came the deeper dive. They had researched my registered LLC for consulting services. They had visited my website, gone through my social media accounts—Facebook, Instagram, Twitter—building a comprehensive picture of my "outside activities."

"We need to understand more about this business," they said, setting up a formal meeting.

THE INTERROGATION

When I walked into that conference room, I knew this wasn't going to be a friendly conversation. There was a whole team of investigators—people whose job it was to dig into employee activities and determine if they violated company policy.

They didn't waste time with pleasantries.

"We've done some research on your business," the lead investigator began, pulling out printed pages from my website and social media accounts. "Your LLC is registered for consulting services. Your website mentions business funding and grants. You've been posting about financial education."

They went through everything methodically. Every post, every page, every mention of my consulting work. It felt like I was being interrogated for a crime rather than having a conversation with my employer.

"We went to your Instagram, your Facebook, your Twitter," another investigator added. "There's a consistent pattern of promoting business services."

The most telling moment came when one of them leaned forward and asked, "If you're making so much money with this daycare and consulting, why are you still working here?"

The question revealed everything about their mindset. In their view, employees should be grateful for their jobs, dependent on the company, completely focused on corporate goals. The idea that someone might have aspirations beyond their role was seen as disloyalty.

I realized then that this investigation wasn't really about company policy or conflicts of interest. It was about control. They wanted employees who needed them completely, who had no other options, who would never dare to walk away.

THE ULTIMATUM

After all that investigation, all those questions and printed screenshots, they gave me their decision: "You have 24 hours to dissolve your LLC. If you do that and provide us with documentation showing it's been dissolved, you can keep your job. Otherwise, we'll have to terminate your employment."

Twenty-four hours to choose between my entrepreneurial dreams and my corporate security.

They also wanted a list of any other LLCs or business entities I owned in any state. "We need complete transparency," they said.

"I'm not doing your job for you," I replied. "If you want to know what else I have, you figure it out."

I left that meeting knowing my time at Wells Fargo was up. There was no way I was dissolving my business to appease a company that saw my ambition as a threat.

But the realization was also liberating in a way. For the first time in years, the choice was clear. I couldn't keep straddling two worlds, trying to be an entrepreneur while remaining a corporate employee. One had to give, and it wasn't going to be my business.

THE WAITING GAME

The weeks between that ultimatum and my actual termination were surreal. I knew what was coming, but life had to go on. I still had sales goals to meet, clients to serve, responsibilities to fulfill.

During this period, they began nitpicking everything I did. When you're working from home, as I was by then, it's easy for managers to find fault if they're looking for it.

"We sent you an email at 2:20, and it's now 2:22. You haven't responded yet." Never mind that I might not have seen it immediately or was in the middle of helping a client.

"On our team call today, everyone else spoke twice, but you only spoke once. We need more active engagement." As if the quality of contribution mattered less than the quantity.

These petty complaints revealed their strategy: build a paper trail to justify the termination they had already decided on. It was death by a thousand cuts, designed to make me look like an underperforming employee rather than someone being fired for entrepreneurial ambition.

THE STRESS MANIFESTED

During those final months at Wells Fargo, my body began rebelling against the stress. I developed severe migraines—the kind that would send me to dark rooms for hours, unable to function. I had to get FMLA (Family and Medical Leave Act) protection because the headaches were so debilitating.

Looking back, I can see clearly that those migraines were my body's way of telling me what my mind refused to acknowledge: this situation was literally making me sick.

It's amazing how the human body responds to chronic stress and misalignment. Since leaving Wells Fargo, I've had maybe one migraine. The headaches that once dominated my life virtually disappeared when I removed myself from that toxic environment.

But at the time, I just took the pain medication and pushed through, telling myself I had to endure it for my family's financial security.

THE LESSONS LEARNED

My fifteen years at Wells Fargo taught me valuable lessons about business, relationships, and personal resilience. I learned how to exceed expectations in challenging environments, how to build trust with clients, how to find opportunities where others saw obstacles.

I also learned to recognize red flags in organizational culture. When a company sees employee ambition as a threat rather than an asset, when they punish success that happens outside their walls, when they demand complete dependence as proof of loyalty—these are signs of an unhealthy workplace.

Most importantly, I learned that security and safety are not the same thing. The job felt secure—steady paycheck, benefits, clear expectations. But it wasn't safe for my mental health, my personal growth, or my long-term aspirations.

Real security comes from developing skills, building relationships, and creating value that transcends any single employer. Real security means having options, not being trapped by dependence.

THE CORPORATE CONTRADICTION

One of the most frustrating aspects of my Wells Fargo experience was the contradiction between what they said they valued and how they actually behaved.

On one hand, they promoted innovation, entrepreneurial thinking, and going above and beyond for clients. They wanted employees who were proactive, creative, problem-solvers.

On the other hand, when I demonstrated these qualities by building my own business, they saw it as a threat. They wanted entrepreneurial thinking, but only in service of their goals. They wanted innovation, but only within their narrow parameters.

This contradiction exists in many corporate environments. Companies want the benefits of entrepreneurial employees—the drive, creativity, and initiative—without accepting the natural conclusion of entrepreneurial thinking: the desire for independence and ownership.

It's an unsustainable model, especially as more people recognize that traditional employment offers less security than it once did. Companies that try to control their employees' entrepreneurial aspirations will increasingly find themselves losing their best talent to those who embrace and support side businesses.

THE SKILL DEVELOPMENT

Despite my growing frustration with Wells Fargo's culture, I can't deny that those fifteen years developed skills that serve me well today.

I learned how to build relationships quickly and authentically. Banking is fundamentally a relationship business—people do business with people they trust. The ability to connect with strangers, understand their needs, and provide solutions is invaluable in any entrepreneurial venture.

I learned how to handle rejection and persist through challenges. Not every client said yes, not every month met quota, not every initiative succeeded. But I learned to see rejection as information rather than judgment, to adjust my approach and keep moving forward.

I learned how to communicate complex financial concepts in simple terms. This skill has been crucial in my grant consulting work, where I need to help entrepreneurs understand funding opportunities and requirements clearly.

I learned how to identify opportunities that others missed. Whether it was the struggling branch that could be turned around or the casual conversation that led to a million-dollar deal, I developed an eye for potential where others saw problems.

Most importantly, I learned what I was capable of achieving when I fully committed to something. The success I had at Wells Fargo—even in difficult circumstances—gave me confidence that I could succeed in my own business as well.

THE WRITING ON THE WALL

By the time that final conversation happened, the writing had been on the wall for months. Wells Fargo had made it clear that they saw my entrepreneurial activities as incompatible with my role as their employee.

But here's what I wish I had understood earlier: their discomfort with my ambition said more about them than it did about me.

A secure, forward-thinking organization would have found ways to leverage my entrepreneurial skills and energy. They might have offered me a role in business development, or created opportunities for me to share my expertise with other clients, or simply celebrated the fact that their employee was successful enough to build something on the side.

Instead, they chose control over creativity, dependence over development.

That choice cost them a high-performing employee who had consistently exceeded expectations. More importantly, it revealed the fundamental limitation of their corporate culture.

PREPARING FOR FREEDOM

In the months leading up to my termination, I began mentally preparing for independence. Not because I was ready—financially or emotionally—but because the alternative was no longer viable.

I started thinking about what I would do if I couldn't rely on that Wells Fargo paycheck. How would I keep the daycare afloat? How would I support my daughter? What resources were available to me?

These weren't comfortable thoughts, but they were necessary ones. Sometimes we need external pressure to push us toward changes we should have made voluntarily.

Looking back, I can see that Wells Fargo was actually doing me a favor. By making my position untenable, they forced me to confront the gap between my comfort zone and my potential.

They pushed me toward a freedom I probably wouldn't have chosen on my own—at least not then.

YOUR CORPORATE EXPERIENCE

As you read this chapter, I want you to think about your own relationship with traditional employment. Whether you're currently in a corporate role, considering leaving one, or have already made the transition to entrepreneurship, there are lessons here for you.

If you're still employed while building a business, pay attention to your company's culture around side ventures. Are they supportive or suspicious? Do they see your entrepreneurial energy as an asset or a threat? Their response will tell you a lot about whether you can successfully build something while remaining an employee.

If you're feeling trapped in a corporate role, consider what skills you're developing that could serve you in your own business. Every job teaches us something, even if it's what we don't want to do with our lives.

And if you've already left corporate America, remember that your employment experience—positive or negative—has prepared you for entrepreneurship in ways you might not fully appreciate yet.

The skills, relationships, and credibility you developed as an employee are assets you can leverage as an entrepreneur. Your understanding of how organizations work, how decisions get made, how relationships matter— all of this knowledge serves you well when you're building your own business or applying for grants.

In the next chapter, we'll explore the parallel path I was walking during those final years at Wells Fargo—building a childcare business while trying to maintain my corporate career. We'll look at the challenges of juggling multiple responsibilities and what I learned about balancing motherhood, employment, and entrepreneurship.

But before we move on, take a moment to appreciate your own corporate experience, whatever it was. Even if it ended badly, even if you were undervalued or mistreated, you survived it. You learned from it. And now you can use those lessons to build something better.

Your corporate years weren't a waste of time—they were preparation for what comes next.

CHAPTER 3

THE PARALLEL PATH

"I don't want to work at a daycare. It takes up all your time."

My daughter's words hit me harder than any performance review or corporate ultimatum ever could. Here I was, thinking I was building something for our future, creating flexibility and freedom through entrepreneurship, and my own child was telling me that my business was stealing me away from her.

It was a moment of reckoning that forced me to confront a painful truth: you can work twice as hard and still end up with less of what you actually want.

Running a childcare center while maintaining my banking career wasn't just challenging—it was a masterclass in the brutal realities of juggling multiple responsibilities. But it also taught me lessons about business, persistence, and priorities that I couldn't have learned any other way.

THE BIRTH OF AN IDEA

The idea for the childcare center didn't come from some grand entrepreneurial vision. It came from a problem I couldn't solve: finding quality, affordable childcare with extended hours for my daughter.

I was a single working mother with a demanding job at Wells Fargo. Most daycare centers closed at 6 PM, but my banking schedule was unpredictable. I might have evening client meetings, weekend events, or extended hours during busy periods. I needed childcare that could accommodate the reality of my professional life, not just standard business hours.

When I looked around, I couldn't find what I needed. The quality centers were expensive and inflexible. The affordable options had limited hours or questionable standards. I was constantly stressed about pickup times, feeling guilty about asking for extensions, and worried about my daughter's care and education.

That's when the daycare my daughter was attending announced they were closing.

The director was amazing with children—truly gifted at creating a nurturing, educational environment. But she struggled with the business side of operations. The finances were a mess, the administrative systems were inadequate, and she was burning out trying to manage both education and business functions.

I saw an opportunity. What if we partnered? She could focus on what she did best—caring for and educating children—while I handled the business operations. My finance background from Wells Fargo would help with budgets, cash flow, and compliance. Her expertise would ensure the children received excellent care.

It seemed like a perfect solution.

THE HARSH REALITY OF STARTUPS

What I didn't realize when I jumped into the childcare business was how much I didn't know about running a business—any business, but especially one with such complex regulations and requirements.

Childcare centers aren't just about watching kids. You need licensing from the state, which involves extensive background checks, facility inspections, and ongoing compliance monitoring. You need to maintain specific teacher-to-child ratios, which means having enough qualified staff even when enrollment fluctuates. You need insurance, curriculum development, meal planning, emergency procedures, and a dozen other systems most people never think about.

We opened our doors with just two children—my daughter and one other child. But the state required us to have a minimum number of employees to operate legally. So there I was, paying five staff members to care for two children. The math was brutal.

Every day that we didn't have more children was a day of significant financial loss. I was essentially paying for the privilege of operating a business with no revenue. My Wells Fargo paycheck wasn't supplementing the business—it was keeping the business alive.

Fortunately, one of my coworkers at the bank had gained custody of four children from a relative, and she brought them all to our center. Suddenly, we went from two to six children, plus my daughter made seven. The additional children from referrals brought us to nine kids, and things started looking more promising.

THE GRIND

Running both businesses simultaneously meant I was essentially working two full-time jobs. My typical day looked like this:

7:00 AM - 5:00 PM: Wells Fargo, dealing with clients, sales goals, meetings, and the increasing pressure around my "outside activities."

5:30 PM - 8:00 PM: Childcare center, handling administrative tasks, talking with parents, managing staff issues, and spending time with the children.

8:30 PM - 10:00 PM: Home with my daughter for homework, dinner, and whatever quality time we could squeeze in before bed.

Then the cycle would start all over again.

Weekends weren't much better. I'd spend Saturdays catching up on daycare paperwork, marketing the business to attract new families, and handling maintenance issues. Sundays were for family time, but even then, I was often fielding calls from parents or dealing with business emergencies.

I was exhausted, stressed, and increasingly aware that something had to give.

The irony wasn't lost on me. I had started the childcare center partly to create more flexibility and freedom in my life. Instead, I had created a situation where I was working more hours than ever before, with more stress and less time with my daughter.

THE MARKETING HUSTLE

One advantage I had in promoting the childcare center was my network at Wells Fargo. Banking put me in contact with working professionals who needed quality childcare—exactly my target market.

I wasn't shy about letting my colleagues know about the center. During conversations about work-life balance, I'd mention our extended hours and flexible policies. When people complained about their current childcare situations, I'd share how we were trying to do things differently.

This wasn't some elaborate marketing strategy—it was just natural conversation. But it was effective. Several of my Wells Fargo colleagues brought their children to our center, and their referrals brought in additional families.

Looking back, this was probably one of the things that raised red flags with Wells Fargo management. They saw me promoting my business within their network and viewed it as using company resources for personal gain. From my perspective, I was just having normal conversations with colleagues who happened to need the services I provided.

This tension—between natural networking and perceived exploitation—is something many employees-turned-entrepreneurs struggle with. Where's the line between sharing information and inappropriately using company relationships? It's a gray area that many companies resolve by simply prohibiting any outside business activities.

THE REGULATORY NIGHTMARE

Just when the childcare center was hitting its stride, the rules changed.

State regulations around childcare are constantly evolving, often in response to incidents or new research about child development. What had worked when we opened suddenly wasn't compliant with new requirements.

The teacher-to-child ratio requirements were adjusted, meaning we needed more qualified staff for the same number of children. The requirements for accepting state funding—which provided steady, guaranteed income for serving low-income families—became more stringent.

The curriculum requirements were updated, necessitating new materials and additional training for our staff. The facility standards were modified, requiring expensive upgrades to our physical space.

Each change individually might have been manageable, but together they created a perfect storm that threatened the viability of our business.

This is one of the harsh realities of certain industries: you can do everything right, build a successful operation, and still face existential threats from regulatory changes you can't control or predict.

THE FINANCIAL SQUEEZE

As regulations tightened and costs increased, our profit margins evaporated. What had been a promising business became a financial drain.

My Wells Fargo paycheck, which I had hoped would be supplemental income, became essential for keeping the daycare afloat. I was essentially subsidizing the business with my corporate salary—the exact opposite of what I had intended.

We had several options:

1. Raise our rates to cover increased costs, potentially losing families who couldn't afford higher fees
2. Reduce our staff, which could compromise the quality of care
3. Stop accepting state funding, losing guaranteed income but avoiding some compliance costs
4. Close the business and cut our losses

None of these options were appealing. Raising rates felt like betraying our mission of providing affordable childcare. Reducing staff could put children at risk and destroy our reputation. Losing state funding would eliminate a significant revenue stream. And closing felt like giving up on something we had worked so hard to build.

So we did what many struggling business owners do: we tried to push through, hoping things would improve.

THE WAKE-UP CALL

The moment that really opened my eyes to what I was sacrificing came during a casual conversation with my daughter. She was about five or six years old at the time, and I was feeling optimistic about the business despite our challenges.

"You know, one day this daycare could be yours," I told her, imagining a future where I could pass down a successful business to the next generation. "When you get older, you could run it."

Her response was immediate and devastating: "I don't want to work at a daycare. It takes up all your time."

Out of the mouths of babes.

I sat there, stunned by the clarity of her observation. My daughter had been watching me work myself to exhaustion, missing bedtime stories and weekend activities because I was always at the daycare or dealing with business issues. She had seen me choose work over presence, task completion over quality time.

The business I had started to create more freedom for our family was actually making me less available to the person who mattered most.

That night, I lay awake thinking about what kind of life I was modeling for my daughter. I was showing her that success meant constant work, that building something meant sacrificing everything else, that business owners don't get to have boundaries or personal time.

These weren't the lessons I wanted to teach her.

THE SYSTEMS PROBLEM

One of the biggest mistakes I made with the childcare center was assuming that my finance background from Wells Fargo had prepared me to run any business. I understood cash flow, budgeting, and basic business principles, but I had no idea how to create the systems and processes necessary for smooth operations.

At Wells Fargo, the systems already existed. I knew exactly what needed to be done each day, how to measure success, and what resources were available to help me achieve my goals. The procedures were documented, the technology was provided, and support staff handled administrative tasks.

Running my own business meant creating all of those systems from scratch.

I needed enrollment procedures, staff scheduling systems, parent communication protocols, emergency procedures, meal planning processes, supply ordering systems, and countless other operational elements that I had taken for granted in my corporate role.

Without proper systems, I was constantly putting out fires instead of building the business. I was reactive rather than proactive, always one step behind instead of strategically planning ahead.

This is a common challenge for people transitioning from employment to entrepreneurship. We assume that being good at our job means we'll be good at running a business. But being an excellent employee and being an effective business owner require different skill sets.

THE NETWORKING STRATEGY

Despite the operational challenges, I did learn valuable lessons about marketing and networking during this period. The success I had promoting the daycare through my Wells Fargo connections taught me the power of relationship-based marketing.

I made it my business to know everyone in the area—not just potential customers, but other business owners, community leaders, and service providers. I attended chamber of commerce events, joined local business groups, and participated in community activities.

This approach served me well both for the daycare and later for my grant consulting business. I learned that people do business with people they know and trust, and that authentic relationships are the foundation of sustainable business growth.

I also learned to be genuinely helpful without immediately expecting something in return. I'd refer potential clients to other business owners, share resources and information, and offer assistance whenever possible. This generosity came back to me many times over in the form of referrals and recommendations.

THE CORPORATE PUSHBACK

As the daycare began attracting more families—many of them through my Wells Fargo network—the bank's attitude toward my side business began to shift.

What had initially been casual questions about my Facebook posts became more serious inquiries about potential conflicts of interest. They started monitoring my social media more closely, looking for evidence that I was using company resources or relationships for personal gain.

The truth is, I was using my network to promote the business. But I wasn't doing anything unethical or inappropriate. I was having natural conversations with colleagues about a service I provided that met their needs.

Still, I could feel the tension building. There were subtle comments about employees who were "too focused" on outside activities. There were new policies about social media use and external business interests. There were reminders about company loyalty and dedication.

The message was clear: Wells Fargo wanted employees who were completely focused on their corporate roles, with no divided loyalties or competing interests.

THE BUSINESS BANKING MISTAKE

One decision that came back to haunt me was banking the daycare's business with Wells Fargo. It seemed logical at the time—I was an employee, I knew the systems, and it felt like it would be convenient to have everything in one place.

What I didn't anticipate was how this would give the bank intimate access to my business finances, allowing them to monitor my revenue, analyze my cash flow, and question my business model.

When Wells Fargo's investigators wanted to understand my childcare business, they didn't need to request financial statements—they could just pull up my account activity. They could see exactly how much money was coming in and going out, which gave them ammunition for their interrogation.

"If you're making so much money with this daycare, why are you still working here?" they asked, as if success in one area should eliminate my desire for stability in another.

This experience taught me the importance of keeping business and personal banking separate, and especially keeping them separate from any employer relationships. Even when there's nothing inappropriate happening, the appearance of transparency can be used against you.

THE IDENTITY CRISIS

Juggling both roles created an identity crisis that I didn't fully recognize at the time. At Wells Fargo, I was Jekwenta the banker—professional, focused, goal-oriented. At the daycare, I was Jekwenta the business owner—creative, nurturing, community-focused.

These weren't necessarily conflicting identities, but they required different mindsets and approaches. The banking world valued conformity, process adherence, and individual achievement. The childcare world valued creativity, collaboration, and community impact.

Switching between these modes throughout each day was mentally and emotionally exhausting. I was constantly adjusting my communication style, my priorities, and my problem-solving approaches based on which role I was playing at any given moment.

This experience taught me the importance of authentic self-expression in work. When you can be yourself—fully yourself—in your professional life, everything becomes easier and more sustainable.

THE LESSON IN PRIORITIES

Perhaps the most important lesson from this period was about priorities and boundaries. I had convinced myself that working harder was the solution to every problem. If the daycare was struggling, I'd work more hours. If Wells Fargo was demanding more, I'd sacrifice personal time to meet their expectations.

But working harder without working smarter is a recipe for burnout and diminishing returns. More hours don't always lead to better results, and constantly being "on" doesn't create the space needed for strategic thinking and creative problem-solving.

My daughter's comment about the daycare taking up all my time forced me to confront a fundamental question: What was the point of building something if it cost me the relationships and experiences that made life worth living?

This realization would become crucial later, when I was building my grant consulting business. I was determined not to repeat the same mistakes— to create a business that enhanced my life rather than consuming it.

THE FOUNDATION FOR WHAT'S NEXT

Despite all the challenges, stress, and eventual struggles of the daycare, this experience was invaluable preparation for my future as an entrepreneur and grant consultant.

I learned firsthand about the regulatory complexities that small businesses face, which helped me better understand the challenges my future clients would encounter. I experienced the cash flow pressures that keep business owners awake at night, giving me empathy for their situations.

I discovered the power of community networking and relationship-based marketing, skills that would become essential for building my consulting practice. I learned to navigate the tensions between multiple priorities and competing demands on my time and energy.

Most importantly, I learned that entrepreneurship isn't just about having a good idea or working hard—it's about creating systems, managing resources, and making difficult decisions under pressure.

This experience also planted the seeds for my later discovery of grants. The financial pressures we faced at the daycare, the frustration with traditional funding options, and the search for alternatives all prepared me to recognize the opportunity that grants represented.

YOUR PARALLEL PATH

Many of you reading this are probably walking your own parallel path right now. You might be building a side business while maintaining your day job, juggling multiple responsibilities and feeling the tension between security and growth.

Here's what I wish I had known during my daycare years:

Set clear boundaries. Define specific hours for each role and protect them fiercely. Don't let one area consistently consume time allocated for another.

Focus on systems over hustle. Working harder isn't always the answer. Sometimes you need to step back and create better processes rather than just putting in more hours.

Separate your finances. Keep business and personal finances completely separate, and definitely don't bank with your employer if you're building a side business.

Communicate your value carefully. Be mindful of how you discuss your entrepreneurial activities with colleagues and supervisors. What feels like natural conversation to you might be perceived as divided loyalty by others.

Remember your why. Regularly check in with your motivations and priorities. If your business is supposed to create more freedom but is actually creating more stress, something needs to change.

Plan your transition. Start thinking about how and when you might transition from employee to full-time entrepreneur. Having a plan reduces anxiety and helps you make strategic decisions.

The parallel path is challenging, but it's also preparation. Every difficulty you face, every skill you develop, every relationship you build is preparing you for the next phase of your journey.

In my case, the struggles with the daycare, the tensions with Wells Fargo, and the impossible juggling act were all leading to something I couldn't yet see: my eventual discovery of grants and my calling as an educator and funding expert.

Your struggles are preparing you for something too. Trust the process, learn from the challenges, and keep moving forward.

In the next chapter, we'll explore what happened when the parallel path became unsustainable—when Wells Fargo forced me to choose between my corporate career and my entrepreneurial dreams, and how that choice led to the most transformative period of my life.

CHAPTER 4

THE BREAKING POINT

"**H**ey, Jekwenta, can we schedule a call at 8:15?"

I stared at my manager's email on the screen, my stomach already knowing what my mind was trying to deny. Our normal team meeting wasn't until 8:30. She wanted to talk to me alone first.

I didn't respond immediately. Instead, I sat there in my home office, looking out the window at a Tuesday morning that felt like any other day but would end up changing everything.

Then the instant message popped up: "Hey, Jekwenta, I see that you're online. Did you see my email about the call at 8:15?"

"Yeah, I'll be on," I typed back.

And just like that, I knew my fifteen-year corporate career was about to end.

THE MORNING THAT CHANGED EVERYTHING

Looking back, I should have seen it coming. The signs had been building for months. The nitpicking, the investigations, the ultimatum to dissolve my LLC. Wells Fargo had made it clear that they saw my entrepreneurial activities as incompatible with my employment.

But knowing something intellectually and experiencing it emotionally are two different things entirely.

When that call came through at 8:15 AM sharp, I picked up with a calmness that surprised even me. Maybe it was resignation. Maybe it was relief. Or maybe it was the part of me that had been preparing for this moment longer than I cared to admit.

"Good morning, Jekwenta," my manager began, her voice carrying that formal tone that managers use when they're about to deliver bad news. "I'm calling to inform you that we're terminating your employment, effective immediately."

There it was. Fifteen years reduced to a single sentence.

She continued with the standard corporate script about final paychecks, benefits continuation, and returning company property. I heard the words but felt strangely detached from them, like I was watching someone else's life unfold.

When she finished, I did something that probably surprised her: I laughed.

"They finally got me," I said, more to myself than to her.

It wasn't a bitter laugh or a hysterical one. It was the laugh of someone who had been holding their breath for months and could finally exhale.

THE IMMEDIATE AFTERMATH

After hanging up, I sat in my home office for several minutes, just processing what had happened. The laptop that had been my window into the corporate world was already locked out of all systems. The email account that had dominated my mornings was gone. The sales goals that had driven my daily schedule were suddenly irrelevant.

I was free.

And I was terrified.

Because freedom, I quickly realized, comes with a price that extends far beyond the obvious financial implications.

That Wells Fargo paycheck wasn't just income—it was my safety net. It was what kept the mortgage current when the daycare had a slow month. It was what allowed me to make payroll when enrollment dipped. It was the stable foundation that made my entrepreneurial risks feel manageable.

Without it, everything felt suddenly, frighteningly uncertain.

THE PERFECT STORM

What made this period even more challenging was that getting fired wasn't happening in isolation. Life has a way of piling on challenges all at once, testing your resilience when you're already stretched thin.

Around the same time as my termination, I was dealing with legal complications from a relationship that had gone bad. The person I had been dating found himself in serious legal trouble—federal trouble—and that created ripple effects that touched every aspect of my life.

The federal investigators didn't just want to understand his business activities; they wanted to understand mine too. They came knocking on my door with questions about the daycare, about my assets, about my income sources. They wanted to make sure I wasn't involved in anything inappropriate or illegal.

I wasn't, of course. But having to lawyer up and deal with federal investigators while simultaneously losing my primary source of income created a level of stress I had never experienced before.

Bills were piling up. Legal fees were mounting. The daycare was struggling with its own financial challenges. And now I had no corporate salary to help keep everything afloat.

It was like watching dominoes fall in slow motion, each challenge triggering the next in a cascade of complications I felt powerless to stop.

THE ISOLATION

One of the hardest parts of this period was how isolated I felt. When you're going through multiple crises simultaneously, it's difficult to know who to turn to for support.

My mother, bless her heart, has always been my backbone. She's the person who will do whatever needs to be done to help me succeed. But she had worked the same job for 35 years and couldn't understand why I would risk everything for entrepreneurship.

When I called to tell her about the termination, her reaction was exactly what I expected and exactly what I didn't need to hear.

"Oh my God," she said, the distress clear in her voice. "You need to start putting in job applications right now. You don't want that termination on your record. I told you a long time ago you should have been looking for work."

Her concern came from a place of love, but it reflected a fundamental difference in how we viewed career and security. To her, a job was safety. To me, it had become a cage.

Her advice to immediately start job hunting felt like being told to run back into a burning building because it was the only shelter I had ever known.

THE MONEY REALITY

Let's talk about the brutal financial reality of getting fired while running a struggling business.

My daycare wasn't generating enough profit to support my lifestyle. The regulatory changes had squeezed our margins to almost nothing. We were barely breaking even on our best months and losing money on the worst ones.

Without my Wells Fargo salary, I couldn't make the mortgage payment. I couldn't cover my personal expenses. I couldn't help keep the daycare operational during slow periods.

I had maxed out credit cards trying to keep everything afloat. I had applied for a loan from Wells Fargo while I still worked there and been declined—a humiliation that stung even more in retrospect.

For the first time in my adult life, I was facing the real possibility of losing everything I had worked for. The house I had bought as a symbol of success. The business I had sacrificed so much to build. The financial stability I thought I had secured.

The American dream I had been chasing was crumbling, and I had to face the possibility that I might not be able to put it back together.

THE LEGAL PRESSURE

Adding to the financial stress was the ongoing legal situation. Having federal investigators interested in your life is expensive, even when you've done nothing wrong.

I had to hire an attorney to represent my interests and ensure that my cooperation with their investigation didn't inadvertently create problems for me. Legal fees start accumulating quickly when you're dealing with federal matters, and every consultation, every document review, every phone call adds to the mounting expenses.

The investigators wanted to understand my business model, my income sources, my financial relationships. They asked detailed questions about how I funded the daycare, where my clients came from, how I managed the business finances.

These weren't accusations—they were trying to piece together a complete picture of the situation. But being under federal scrutiny while simultaneously losing your primary income creates a level of anxiety that's hard to describe.

Every phone call could be important. Every document request had to be taken seriously. Every meeting required careful preparation and legal counsel.

It was exhausting, expensive, and emotionally draining.

THE IDENTITY CRISIS

Getting fired forces you to confront questions about yourself that you might prefer to avoid.

For fifteen years, a significant part of my identity had been tied to my role at Wells Fargo. I was Jekwenta the banker, the high performer, the woman who could turn around struggling branches and close million-dollar deals.

Suddenly, I was just Jekwenta the unemployed single mother with a failing business and mounting legal bills.

Who was I without that corporate title? What was I worth without that steady paycheck? What did I have to offer the world if I couldn't even keep my own financial house in order?

These are brutal questions that every fired employee faces, but they're especially acute when you're also dealing with other major life challenges.

I had always prided myself on being independent, on being able to handle whatever life threw at me. But this situation was testing the limits of my resilience and self-reliance.

THE SUPPORT SYSTEM CHALLENGE

During crisis periods, you learn a lot about your relationships and support systems. You discover who shows up when times are tough and who disappears when you need them most.

Some relationships surprised me. People I had considered close friends seemed uncomfortable with my situation and gradually pulled away. Whether it was the legal complications, the financial stress, or just the general messiness of my life, they preferred to keep their distance.

But other relationships deepened. A few friends stepped up in ways I hadn't expected, offering practical help, emotional support, and encouragement when I needed it most.

The challenge was learning to accept help when I had always been the one helping others. My independent streak made it difficult to acknowledge that I needed support, let alone ask for it.

This period taught me that accepting help isn't a sign of weakness—it's a necessary part of navigating major life transitions. And the people who love you want to help, but they need permission to do so.

THE SLEEPLESS NIGHTS

Nothing reveals your anxieties like financial pressure and uncertainty about the future.

I spent countless nights lying awake, running scenarios in my head. How long could I survive without income? What would happen if I couldn't make the mortgage payment? Should I close the daycare and cut my losses? Should I swallow my pride and start applying for corporate jobs?

Each option seemed to come with significant downsides. Closing the daycare meant admitting failure and disappointing the families who depended on us. Going back to corporate employment meant accepting that my entrepreneurial dreams weren't viable.

But doing nothing meant watching everything fall apart in slow motion.

The mental gymnastics of trying to solve unsolvable problems was exhausting. I'd fall asleep thinking about one approach and wake up at 3 AM with a completely different plan, only to realize its flaws by morning.

This kind of stress takes a physical toll. I was tired all the time but couldn't rest deeply. I was hungry but couldn't eat properly. I was social but felt isolated even in crowds.

THE MOMENT OF TRUTH

About a month into unemployment, I had to face some hard truths about my situation.

The daycare wasn't going to suddenly become profitable enough to support my lifestyle. The legal situation wasn't going to resolve quickly or cheaply. And my savings weren't going to last much longer.

I could either panic and make desperate decisions, or I could get strategic about finding solutions.

That's when I remembered something that had been mentioned to me several times but that I had always dismissed: grants.

The woman who handled our daycare certifications had mentioned grants repeatedly. "Girl, you need to apply for grants," she'd say. And every time, I'd brush her off. "I ain't got time for that."

But now I had nothing but time. And I was desperate enough to try anything.

I had always assumed grants were only for nonprofits. I thought you needed special training or certification to apply. I figured the process was too complicated for someone like me to navigate.

But what did I have to lose? My business was struggling anyway. My traditional funding sources had been exhausted. And I was running out of options.

So I started researching grants. Not with any great optimism or expectation of success. Just with the desperate hope that maybe, possibly, there was something out there that could help.

THE SILVER LINING

Looking back now, I can see that getting fired was the best thing that ever happened to me professionally. But I couldn't see that at the time.

At the time, it felt like failure. It felt like everything I had worked for was falling apart. It felt like I was letting down everyone who depended on me—my daughter, my daycare families, my employees.

But sometimes what feels like an ending is actually a beginning. Sometimes what looks like failure is actually redirection. Sometimes what seems like the worst thing that could happen is actually the push you needed to discover what you were really meant to do.

The termination from Wells Fargo forced me to confront the gap between my comfort zone and my potential. It pushed me to explore funding sources I had never considered. It made me resourceful in ways I had never needed to be.

Most importantly, it gave me the freedom to fully commit to building something of my own. As long as I had that corporate paycheck, I could always fall back on it when entrepreneurship got difficult. Without it, I had to make my business work or face serious consequences.

That pressure, as uncomfortable as it was, became fuel for innovation and persistence.

THE LESSON IN RESILIENCE

This period taught me that resilience isn't about avoiding difficulties—it's about learning to navigate them effectively.

I couldn't control getting fired. I couldn't control the legal complications. I couldn't control the regulatory changes that hurt my daycare. But I could control how I responded to these challenges.

I could choose to see problems as permanent or temporary. I could choose to view setbacks as evidence of personal failure or as information about what wasn't working. I could choose to isolate myself or reach out for support.

These choices didn't make the difficulties disappear, but they determined whether I would emerge from this period stronger or weaker, wiser or more bitter, more resourceful or more defeated.

The challenges were real, and the stress was overwhelming at times. But hidden within the crisis were opportunities I couldn't have accessed any other way.

YOUR BREAKING POINT

If you're reading this book, you might be approaching or experiencing your own breaking point. Maybe you've been fired or laid off. Maybe your business is struggling. Maybe you're facing multiple challenges that seem to be compounding each other.

Here's what I want you to know: breaking points aren't just about things falling apart. They're also about breakthrough moments that wouldn't be possible any other way.

When your back is against the wall, you discover resources you didn't know you had. When your usual solutions stop working, you're forced to think creatively. When your comfort zone becomes untenable, you're motivated to take risks you would have avoided otherwise.

Your breaking point might be the catalyst for your breakthrough.

But breakthrough requires action. It requires being willing to try things you've never tried before, to ask for help you've never needed, to explore options you've never considered.

For me, that action was researching grants. It was swallowing my pride and admitting that I needed funding I couldn't generate on my own. It was being willing to learn something completely new when I felt like I should already have all the answers.

In the next chapter, I'll take you through that turning point—the moment when desperation led to discovery, when rock bottom became the foundation for something better, and when getting fired into freedom finally started to feel like freedom instead of just getting fired.

But before we move on, I want you to consider this: What if your current challenges aren't punishments but preparations? What if the things that feel like failures are actually redirections toward something better?

What if your breaking point is actually your breakthrough waiting to happen?

CHAPTER 5

THE TURNING POINT

"**G**irl, you need to apply for grants."

How many times had I heard those words? The woman who handled our daycare certifications must have said it to me a dozen times over the years. And every single time, I had the same response: "I ain't got time for that."

But now, sitting in my home office with no corporate job to rush to, no sales goals to meet, and bills piling up faster than I could count them, I finally had something I hadn't had before: time.

And desperation.

Sometimes it takes hitting rock bottom to finally pay attention to the opportunities that have been sitting right in front of you.

THE RESEARCH BEGINS

My journey into the world of grants didn't start with grand ambitions or deep research. It started with a Google search born out of desperation and the fading hope that maybe, just maybe, there was something out there that could help save my struggling daycare.

I had always assumed grants were for nonprofits. I thought you needed to be a certified grant writer or hire an expensive consultant. I figured the application process was so complex that regular business owners like me couldn't navigate it successfully.

But what did I have to lose? My traditional funding sources were exhausted. I had been declined for a loan from my own employer. Credit cards were maxed out. And closing the daycare was starting to look like the only realistic option.

So I started researching.

The more I read, the more I realized how wrong my assumptions had been. There were grants specifically for small businesses. There were foundations that funded childcare centers. There were opportunities for entrepreneurs that I had never known existed.

Most shocking of all, many of these grants didn't require you to pay the money back. They weren't loans with interest rates and monthly payments. They were investments in businesses and ideas that aligned with the funder's mission.

THE FIRST APPLICATION

After days of research, I found a foundation that offered small business grants. The application was straightforward—they wanted to know about my business, what I planned to do with the funding, and how it would impact my community.

I filled out the application honestly, describing our childcare center, the challenges we were facing with regulatory changes, and how additional funding would help us continue serving working families in our area.

The whole process took me less than 30 minutes.

I remember hitting "submit" and feeling a mixture of hope and skepticism. Thirty minutes to potentially save my business? It seemed too good to be true.

But a few weeks later, I received an email that changed everything: "Congratulations, your grant application has been approved for $500."

Five hundred dollars. It wasn't life-changing money, but it was something. More importantly, it was proof that this whole grant thing actually worked.

THE LIGHTBULB MOMENT

As I sat there staring at that approval email, a lightbulb went off in my head.

Wait a minute. All I had to do was tell these people what I wanted to do with the money, spend 30 minutes filling out an application, and they gave me $500?

I could do this all day long.

That $500 grant became the catalyst for everything that followed. Not because of the money itself, but because of what it represented: a completely different approach to business funding that I had never fully understood.

Traditional funding—loans, credit cards, investor capital—is all about proving you can pay money back. You have to demonstrate creditworthiness, provide collateral, or give up equity in your business.

Grants are different. They're about proving you can create value. They're about showing that your business or project aligns with the funder's mission and that their investment will generate positive outcomes.

It's a fundamental shift from "Can you repay us?" to "Can you help us achieve our goals?"

THE LEARNING CURVE

That first $500 grant was just the beginning. I started applying for more grants, learning the system, understanding what different funders were looking for.

Some applications were rejected. That's part of the process. But others were approved, and gradually I began to understand the patterns and principles that led to success.

I learned that positioning matters more than anything else. It's not about how desperately you need the money—it's about how effectively you can use it to solve problems the funder cares about.

I learned that grants are competitive, but most people never even apply because they assume they won't qualify or the process is too difficult.

I learned that there are thousands of funding opportunities out there that most business owners never discover because they don't know where to look or how to search effectively.

Most importantly, I learned that grant applications aren't as complicated as I had thought. They require clear thinking and effective communication, but those are skills most business owners already have—they just don't know how to apply them to grant writing.

THE COMMUNITY RESPONSE

As I started having success with grants and sharing my experiences on social media, something unexpected happened: people began asking how they could do the same thing.

I was posting about my grant wins not to brag, but to document my journey and maybe inspire others who were struggling like I had been. But those posts generated questions and comments from entrepreneurs who had never considered grants as a funding option.

"How did you find that grant?" "What did you say in your application?" "Do you think I could qualify for something like that?" "Could you help me apply for grants?"

I realized that I wasn't the only business owner who had been operating under false assumptions about grants. There were thousands of entrepreneurs out there who could benefit from this funding source but didn't know how to access it.

THE COACHING BEGINS

Initially, I resisted the idea of teaching others about grants. I was still working on my own business challenges, still learning the system myself. Who was I to be coaching other people?

But the requests kept coming. Friends, former colleagues, people in my network—they all wanted to know how to replicate what I was doing.

Finally, I decided to host a free workshop in Nashville. I figured if I was going to answer the same questions over and over, I might as well do it once for a group of people.

I rented space in an empty rental property I owned and invited anyone who was interested in learning about grants to attend. I expected maybe a dozen people to show up.

The room was packed wall to wall.

Then people in Huntsville, where I lived, heard about the Nashville event and asked, "What about us?" So I hosted another free workshop in Huntsville.

Same result—wall to wall attendance.

That's when I realized I had stumbled onto something significant. There was enormous demand for practical, accessible grant education. People were hungry for this information, but they didn't know where to get it.

THE COACH K BRAND

During this period, people started calling me "Coach K." It wasn't a planned branding decision—it just happened naturally.

My name is Jekwenta, but people have trouble pronouncing it. So friends and family have always called me "Quinn" or "Quina." At work, people would come into the bank asking for "the K girl" when they couldn't remember my name.

But after I started helping people with grants and business funding, "Coach K" stuck. People would see me in public and say, "Hey, Coach K, I have a question for you."

The name felt right because it captured what I was becoming: someone who educated and guided others toward their goals rather than doing the work for them.

I could have positioned myself as a grant writer, charging thousands of dollars to write applications for clients with no guarantee of success. Instead, I chose to be an educator, teaching entrepreneurs how to find and win grants themselves.

This decision was partly philosophical—I believe in empowering people with knowledge rather than creating dependence—and partly practical. Grant writers charge $5,000 to $10,000 with no guarantee of results. I couldn't feel good about taking that much money from struggling business owners without being able to promise them at least a $20,000 return.

THE METHODOLOGY DEVELOPS

As I worked with more entrepreneurs and refined my approach, I began to develop a systematic methodology for grant success.

I realized that most people were making the same mistakes: they were positioning themselves as victims needing charity rather than problem-solvers deserving investment. They were focusing on their needs instead of the funder's goals. They were limiting themselves to industry-specific grants instead of thinking broadly about how their business could address various social and economic challenges.

I developed a framework that started with identifying problems within your community or industry and positioning your business as the solution. Instead of saying "I need money to start my business," successful applicants were saying "I have a solution to a problem you care about, and with your funding, I can implement it more effectively."

This shift in thinking—from need-based to value-based positioning— was transformational for my clients.

THE SUCCESS STORIES BEGIN

As my methodology became more refined, the success stories started accumulating.

Kathy was one of my first major success stories. She came to me with no background in grant writing and a for-profit business that she wasn't sure would qualify for grants. Within 90 days of implementing my approach, she was approved for her first grant of $15,000.

But she didn't stop there. She started a nonprofit organization and got that approved for $25,000. In less than four months, she had secured $40,000 in funding just by executing on the information I had taught her.

Then there was Emma, who has now received nearly a million dollars in grant funding using my methods. And Megan, who sits at home applying for grants and has secured $2.6 million across three different organizations.

These weren't exceptional cases or people with special advantages. They were regular entrepreneurs who followed a proven process and didn't give up when faced with initial rejections.

THE REALIZATION

Somewhere during this period, I had a profound realization about my journey. Getting fired from Wells Fargo hadn't been a setback—it had been a setup.

Everything that had seemed like failure or misfortune was actually preparing me for this moment. My finance background gave me credibility when talking about business funding. My experience with the struggling daycare helped me understand the challenges my clients were facing. My corporate network provided initial clients and testimonials.

Even the legal complications and financial stress of that difficult period served a purpose. They gave me empathy for entrepreneurs facing their own crises and urgency around finding funding solutions.

I had been so focused on what I was losing that I couldn't see what I was being prepared to gain.

THE MISSION EMERGES

As my coaching practice grew and I saw the transformative impact grants could have on people's lives and businesses, a larger mission began to emerge.

I wasn't just helping individual entrepreneurs secure funding. I was democratizing access to capital. I was challenging the narrative that only certain types of businesses or certain types of people deserve investment.

The traditional funding landscape—banks, venture capital, angel investors—has significant barriers and biases. Grants represent a different model, one based on value creation and social impact rather than just profit potential and personal connections.

My goal became bigger than just teaching grant applications. I wanted to become the "Earn Your Leisure of grants"—the go-to resource for entrepreneurs who needed funding education and empowerment.

I wanted to knock down the doors of corporations and foundations and tell them that minority-owned businesses and women-owned businesses deserve capital not because of charity or diversity initiatives, but because they have structured companies providing resources and opportunities to their communities.

THE FREEDOM BEGINS

As my grant consulting business grew and became profitable, I began to experience something I had been chasing for years: real freedom.

Not the illusion of security that came with a corporate paycheck, but the genuine freedom that comes from building something valuable, sustainable, and aligned with your values.

I could set my own schedule, prioritizing time with my daughter in ways that had been impossible when I was juggling banking and the daycare. I could choose which clients to work with and which projects to pursue. I could say no to opportunities that didn't align with my mission.

Most importantly, I could see the direct connection between my work and its impact. Every client who secured funding, every entrepreneur who gained confidence, every business that was able to grow because of grants I helped them win—these were tangible results that made every difficult moment of the journey worthwhile.

THE FULL CIRCLE MOMENT

One of the most satisfying aspects of this transformation was how it connected back to my earliest career experiences.

Remember that moment at Advance America when I showed a customer how much she had paid in fees over the years, and she broke down crying? That was the first time I truly understood the devastating impact of financial illiteracy and predatory systems.

Now I was helping entrepreneurs access funding that didn't have to be paid back, that didn't trap them in cycles of debt, that actually empowered them to build wealth and create opportunities for others.

I had found my way to the other side of the financial education equation. Instead of witnessing how lack of knowledge trapped people, I was teaching knowledge that liberated them.

YOUR TURNING POINT

Every entrepreneur has moments when everything could go either way. When the next decision could lead to breakthrough or breakdown. When desperation could become either paralysis or motivation.

My turning point came when I finally paid attention to advice I had been ignoring for years. When I was desperate enough to try something new. When I was willing to admit that my assumptions might be wrong.

What opportunities have you been ignoring? What advice have you been dismissing? What assumptions about funding, about your qualifications, about your industry might be limiting your options?

Your turning point might be closer than you think. It might be hiding in plain sight, camouflaged as something too simple to be effective or too good to be true.

The key is being willing to try something different when what you've been doing stops working. Being open to information that challenges your preconceptions. Being desperate enough—or courageous enough— to step outside your comfort zone.

In my case, that step led to discovering a funding source that transformed my business and my life. It led to finding my true calling as an educator and empowerment coach. It led to building something that creates value for others while providing freedom for myself.

But it required being willing to start with a single application, to invest 30 minutes in something I didn't fully understand, to trust that maybe— just maybe—there was a better way.

In the next chapter, we'll explore the mindset shifts that had to happen for me to fully embrace this new path. Because discovering grants was just the beginning. The real transformation happened when I learned to think differently about independence, support, and what it means to build something meaningful.

But for now, consider this: What if your next turning point is waiting for you to pay attention to advice you've been ignoring? What if the solution to your current challenges is simpler than you think?

What if your breakthrough is just one application away?

CHAPTER 6

BREAKING THE INDEPENDENCE MYTH

"**W**hy wouldn't you tell me you needed help? I could have helped you."

My father's words cut through me like a knife. Here I was, struggling to keep my business afloat, drowning in bills, and facing the possibility of losing everything I had worked for. And all along, I had people in my life who could have helped—people who wanted to help—but I was too proud to ask.

This conversation happened months into my unemployment, after I had exhausted my savings, maxed out my credit cards, and was seriously considering closing the daycare. My father had no idea how bad things had gotten because I hadn't told him.

In my mind, asking for help would have meant admitting failure. It would have meant acknowledging that I couldn't handle things on my own. It would have made me feel weak, dependent, and somehow less capable.

I was wrong about all of it.

THE SPOILED GIRL'S INDEPENDENCE REBELLION

To understand why asking for help was so difficult for me, you have to understand where I came from.

Growing up as daddy's spoiled girl meant I had always been able to pick up the phone and get whatever I needed. Money for college? Dad handled it. Car trouble? Dad took care of it. Emergency expenses? There was always a safety net.

But when I decided to forge my own path, I went to the opposite extreme. I was determined to prove that I could make it without anyone's help. I wanted to demonstrate that I was independent, self-sufficient, and capable of handling whatever life threw at me.

This wasn't just about money—it was about identity. I needed to know that I could succeed on my own merits, not because of my family's resources or connections.

So when the daycare started struggling, when Wells Fargo began investigating my business activities, when bills started piling up, I didn't reach out. I didn't ask for advice, support, or assistance. I just doubled down on trying to handle everything myself.

Pride, I discovered, can be the most expensive luxury you'll ever own.

THE ISOLATION TRAP

The irony of my independence quest was that it led to the exact opposite of what I was trying to achieve. Instead of proving my strength, it exposed my limitations. Instead of demonstrating my capability, it highlighted areas where I needed help.

When you're struggling alone, every setback feels like personal failure. Every challenge seems insurmountable. Every decision carries the weight of knowing that if you choose wrong, there's no backup plan.

I was trying to be the sole architect, contractor, and laborer of my life, and I was burning out in the process.

Meanwhile, I was surrounded by people with experience, resources, and perspectives that could have made my journey easier. But I had convinced myself that accepting help would somehow diminish my accomplishment.

This is what I call the independence trap: the belief that self-reliance means rejecting all forms of support, guidance, or assistance.

THE WAKE-UP CALL

The conversation with my father was a wake-up call, but it wasn't the first one. There had been signs for months that my approach wasn't working.

I remember sitting in my car in the Wells Fargo parking lot before they fired me, overwhelmed by stress and uncertain about the future. I had my phone in my hand, considering who I could call for advice or support. But I talked myself out of making any calls.

"I need to figure this out myself," I thought. "I don't want to burden anyone with my problems."

Looking back, I can see how backwards that thinking was. The people who care about you want to help when you're struggling. They want to share their knowledge, resources, and networks. They want to see you succeed.

By refusing to reach out, I wasn't protecting them from my problems—I was depriving them of the opportunity to make a difference in my life.

THE GRANT REVELATION

What's fascinating is that grants taught me the lesson I had been resisting in my personal life: asking for support isn't weakness—it's strategy.

When you apply for a grant, you're not begging for charity. You're proposing a partnership. You're saying, "I have a solution to a problem you care about, and with your funding, I can implement it more effectively."

The funder benefits because they get to advance their mission through your work. You benefit because you get the resources needed to create impact. It's a mutually beneficial relationship, not a one-sided dependency.

This realization fundamentally changed how I thought about asking for help in all areas of life.

THE SUPPORT SPECTRUM

I began to understand that there's a spectrum of support, and different situations call for different types of assistance:

Information Support: Sometimes you need knowledge, advice, or guidance from people who have been where you're trying to go.

Emotional Support: Sometimes you need encouragement, validation, or simply someone to listen when you're processing challenges.

Network Support: Sometimes you need introductions, referrals, or access to people and opportunities outside your current circle.

Resource Support: Sometimes you need financial assistance, equipment, or other tangible resources to move forward.

Skill Support: Sometimes you need help with tasks that are outside your expertise or would take you too long to complete effectively.

The key insight was that accepting one type of support doesn't mean you need all types. You can be independent in some areas while getting help in others. You can be self-reliant about certain decisions while seeking input on others.

THE MENTORSHIP GAME-CHANGER

The most transformative support I received was mentorship. When I finally connected with Neo and Marcus from ROI Society, everything changed.

They had already built successful businesses. They understood the challenges I was facing because they had faced similar ones. They could see my blind spots and help me avoid mistakes they had already made.

Most importantly, they could help me think strategically about my business instead of just reactively responding to whatever crisis was happening that week.

With their guidance, my revenue went from barely making $10,000 a month to consistently generating well over $100,000 monthly. But the financial results were just one benefit. The real value was in how they helped me think differently about business, marketing, and scale.

THE SWALLOWING PRIDE QUESTION

After I shared my story at speaking events, people would often ask, "How do you swallow your pride and ask for help?"

The question itself reveals the problem: the assumption that asking for help requires "swallowing pride" rather than exercising wisdom.

Here's what I learned about making this shift:

Find the Right People: Not everyone is equipped to help you, and not everyone who offers help has your best interests at heart. Look for people who have achieved what you're trying to achieve, who understand your industry or challenges, and who communicate in a way that resonates with you.

Reframe the Request: Instead of thinking "I need help because I'm failing," try "I want to accelerate my progress by learning from people who have been where I'm trying to go."

Offer Value in Return: The best mentoring relationships are mutually beneficial. Consider what you can offer—fresh perspectives, assistance with projects, connections to people in your network, or simply genuine appreciation and implementation of their advice.

Start Small: You don't have to share your deepest challenges immediately. Start with specific questions or requests for feedback on particular decisions.

Be Coachable: The fastest way to lose mentoring opportunities is to ask for advice and then argue with it or ignore it. You don't have to implement every suggestion, but you should seriously consider the guidance you receive.

THE ABUNDANCE MINDSET SHIFT

The independence myth is rooted in scarcity thinking: the belief that resources, opportunities, and support are limited, so you have to compete for them or do without them.

Grants helped me develop an abundance mindset: the understanding that there are resources available specifically to help people like me succeed, and that accessing these resources creates value for everyone involved.

This shift affected every aspect of my business and personal life. Instead of hoarding information, I started sharing it freely, knowing that helping others succeed would create more opportunities for everyone. Instead of seeing other grant consultants as competition, I began viewing them as colleagues in a mission to democratize access to funding.

Instead of feeling guilty about my success, I started seeing it as proof of what was possible for others who were willing to learn and apply the same principles.

THE COLLABORATION ADVANTAGE

Once I embraced support and collaboration, I discovered advantages I had never accessed while trying to do everything alone:

Faster Learning: Instead of making every mistake myself, I could learn from others' experiences and avoid predictable pitfalls.

Better Decisions: Having advisors and mentors meant I could get input on important decisions instead of relying solely on my own perspective.

Expanded Networks: Each relationship opened doors to other relationships, creating exponential opportunities for growth and learning.

Emotional Resilience: Having people who understood my challenges and believed in my vision made it easier to persevere through difficult periods.

Skill Amplification: By partnering with people who had complementary skills, I could achieve results that would have been impossible on my own.

Resource Access: Mentors and collaborators often had resources—financial, technological, or informational—that they were willing to share.

THE INDEPENDENCE REDEFINITION

Through this process, I learned to redefine independence. True independence isn't about rejecting all forms of support—it's about having options.

When you have strong relationships, diverse skills, multiple income streams, and access to resources, you're not dependent on any single person or opportunity. You're independent because you have choices.

When you're isolated and trying to do everything yourself, you're actually more vulnerable to setbacks because you don't have backup options or alternative approaches.

Real independence means building a support system so strong that you never have to depend on any single element of it.

THE GIVING BACK IMPERATIVE

As my business grew and I experienced the benefits of support and mentorship, I felt a responsibility to pay it forward.

I started mentoring other entrepreneurs, sharing what I had learned about grants and business building. I created free resources and workshops. I made myself available for questions and guidance from people who were earlier in their journeys.

This wasn't just about karma or giving back—it was strategic. Teaching others reinforced my own learning. Helping entrepreneurs succeed created potential collaborators and referral sources. Building a reputation as someone who genuinely cared about others' success attracted high-quality relationships and opportunities.

The abundance mindset is self-reinforcing: the more you give, the more you receive, which enables you to give even more.

THE FAMILY DYNAMICS

The independence myth also affected my family relationships. My determination to prove myself sometimes created distance between me and the people who loved me most.

My mother, who had worked the same job for 35 years, struggled to understand my entrepreneurial journey. Her advice to immediately start job hunting after I was fired came from a place of love and concern, but it reflected a fundamental difference in how we viewed security and risk.

My father, who had his own entrepreneurial experience, understood my ambitions but was frustrated that I hadn't reached out when I needed help.

Learning to accept support from family members required acknowledging that their concern came from love, not doubt about my capabilities. It meant being vulnerable enough to share my struggles instead of trying to present a perfect facade.

It also meant helping them understand my perspective and goals so they could provide more appropriate support.

THE CLIENT IMPACT

As I integrated these lessons about support and collaboration into my own life, I began teaching them to my grant clients as well.

Many entrepreneurs struggle with the same independence myth that had trapped me. They're hesitant to apply for grants because they see it as asking for handouts. They're reluctant to seek mentorship because they want to prove they can succeed alone.

I help them reframe these attitudes:

Grants aren't charity—they're strategic partnerships with organizations that want to achieve the same outcomes you're working toward.

Mentorship isn't dependency—it's acceleration of your learning and growth process.

Collaboration isn't weakness—it's multiplication of your capabilities and impact.

Support isn't limitation—it's expansion of your options and resources.

This mindset shift often makes the difference between clients who succeed with grants and those who struggle with applications and positioning.

THE TRUST FACTOR

Learning to accept support also taught me about trust—both trusting others and becoming trustworthy myself.

When someone offers guidance, resources, or assistance, they're taking a risk. They're investing their time, reputation, or resources in your success. Honoring that investment by implementing their advice, updating them on results, and expressing genuine appreciation builds trust that can lead to even more support.

Similarly, when I offer support to others, I'm looking for signs that they'll use it wisely and value it appropriately. The entrepreneurs who follow through, report back, and show appreciation are the ones I'm most willing to help repeatedly.

Trust creates upward spirals in relationships, while taking support for granted creates downward spirals.

THE PRACTICAL APPLICATIONS

Here are practical ways to start breaking the independence myth in your own life:

Identify Your Support Needs: Where are you struggling that others could help? What skills, knowledge, or resources would accelerate your progress?

Map Your Network: Who do you already know who might be able to help or connect you with people who can help?

Start Small: Ask for specific, limited assistance rather than broad, open-ended support.

Offer Value First: Look for ways to help others before asking for help yourself.

Be Strategic: Don't ask for help with things you can easily do yourself. Focus on areas where outside input would significantly impact your results.

Follow Through: Implement the advice you receive and report back on results. This builds trust and encourages continued support.

Express Appreciation: Acknowledge the time and effort others invest in your success.

YOUR INDEPENDENCE MYTH

As you read this chapter, consider what independence myths might be limiting your own progress.

Are you avoiding grants because you see them as handouts rather than partnerships?

Are you struggling with challenges that others in your network could easily help you solve?

Are you trying to build everything from scratch instead of learning from people who have already solved similar problems?

Are you defining strength as never needing help rather than as having the wisdom to seek support when it would be beneficial?

The independence myth is seductive because it promises that you can control your outcomes completely. But control is often an illusion, and the attempt to maintain it can actually limit your results.

True strength lies in building relationships, systems, and resources that give you options and opportunities you couldn't create alone.

In the next chapter, we'll explore how shifting from scarcity to abundance thinking affects every aspect of your business and grant applications. We'll look at how to position yourself not as someone who needs charity, but as someone who creates value worthy of investment.

But for now, consider this: What if asking for support isn't a sign that you're not ready for success—what if it's evidence that you are?

CHAPTER 7

FROM SCARCITY TO ABUNDANCE

"I need this grant because my business is struggling and I'm behind on bills."

If I had a dollar for every time I've heard someone position their grant application this way, I could probably fund a few grants myself.

Here's the hard truth: funders don't invest in desperation. They invest in vision.

The shift from scarcity thinking to abundance thinking isn't just about feeling better or being more positive—it's about fundamentally changing how you position yourself in the world. And when it comes to grants, this mindset shift can mean the difference between rejection and approval, between being seen as a charity case and being viewed as a strategic partner.

Let me take you through my own journey from scarcity to abundance, and show you how this transformation didn't just change my grant applications—it changed my entire approach to business and life.

THE SCARCITY STORY

When I first started applying for grants, my mindset was rooted in lack. My business was failing. I was behind on bills. I was running out of options. I needed help, and I needed it fast.

Every grant application I wrote came from this place of desperation:

"Our daycare is struggling due to regulatory changes..." "We need funding to keep our doors open..." "Without this grant, we may have to close..."

I was essentially asking funders to rescue me from my problems. I was positioning myself as a victim of circumstances beyond my control, hoping someone would take pity on my situation.

And you know what happened? I got rejected. A lot.

It took that first $500 approval to help me understand that I had been approaching grants completely backwards.

THE MINDSET REVELATION

That $500 grant wasn't awarded because of my problems—it was awarded because of my solutions.

When I read the approval letter more carefully, I noticed they weren't responding to my struggles. They were excited about what I planned to do with their funding: expand our educational programming, serve more working families, and create jobs in our community.

The funder didn't care that I was having financial difficulties. They cared that their investment would help achieve outcomes they valued.

This was my first glimpse into abundance thinking: instead of focusing on what I lacked, I needed to focus on what I could create.

THE POSITIONING TRANSFORMATION

Once I understood this principle, I completely rewrote my approach to grant applications.

Instead of: "Our daycare is struggling and needs funding to survive."

I wrote: "We have an opportunity to expand quality childcare services for working families while creating educational programming that prepares children for academic success."

Instead of: "We're behind on bills and might have to close."

I wrote: "With additional funding, we can serve 50% more families and hire three additional teachers from our local community."

Instead of: "We need help because things are going badly."

I wrote: "We want to amplify our impact because things are going well."

The facts about my situation hadn't changed. My financial challenges were still real. But my positioning had shifted from scarcity to abundance, from problems to solutions, from desperation to opportunity.

THE ABUNDANCE FRAMEWORK

As I refined this approach, I developed what I now call the Abundance Framework for grant applications:

Problem Identification: Instead of focusing on your problems, identify problems in your community or industry that your business is positioned to solve.

Solution Positioning: Present your business as the solution to these problems, not as a business with problems.

Impact Amplification: Show how funding will allow you to increase your positive impact, not just survive your current challenges.

Community Benefit: Demonstrate how your success creates value for others, not just for yourself.

Future Vision: Paint a picture of what becomes possible with funding, not what disasters you're trying to avoid.

This framework transforms you from a supplicant to a partner, from someone seeking charity to someone offering value.

THE MONEY STORY TRANSFORMATION

My relationship with money had to evolve alongside my grant positioning. Growing up spoiled meant I had a complicated relationship with financial independence.

On one hand, I had always had access to money when I needed it, which created a sense of entitlement and expectation. On the other hand, when I decided to be independent, I swung to the opposite extreme of refusing help and trying to do everything through my own resources.

Both approaches were rooted in scarcity thinking.

The entitlement mindset said: "I deserve money because of who I am."

The independence mindset said: "I can't ask for money because that makes me weak."

Abundance thinking offered a third option: "I can access money because of the value I create."

This shift was liberating. It meant I didn't have to choose between pride and survival. I could seek funding from a position of strength rather than weakness.

THE CLIENT EDUCATION PROCESS

As my grant coaching business grew, I realized that most of my clients were struggling with the same scarcity mindset I had overcome.

They would come to me saying things like:

"I need grants because banks won't lend to me." "I'm a minority-owned business, so I should qualify for funding." "My business is struggling and I'm desperate for help."

While these statements might be factually accurate, they were positioning themselves from scarcity rather than abundance.

I had to help them reframe their stories:

Instead of "Banks won't lend to me," we'd say "I prefer non-debt funding that allows me to maintain full ownership while scaling my impact."

Instead of "I should qualify because I'm a minority," we'd say "My business addresses gaps in services to underserved communities."

Instead of "I'm desperate for help," we'd say "I'm ready to scale solutions that are already working."

THE ENERGY SHIFT

What's fascinating about this mindset transformation is how it affects your energy and presence.

When you're operating from scarcity, you carry a heaviness. You're focused on problems, limitations, and what's not working. You approach conversations with neediness and desperation. People can sense this energy, and it's not attractive to potential funders, partners, or clients.

When you operate from abundance, you carry lightness and possibility. You're focused on solutions, opportunities, and what's working. You approach conversations with confidence and vision. This energy attracts people who want to be part of something successful and impactful.

The shift in energy often precedes the shift in results.

THE COMPETITION REFRAME

Scarcity thinking views grant funding as a zero-sum game: if someone else wins a grant, that means less money is available for you.

Abundance thinking recognizes that successful grant recipients actually create more funding opportunities for everyone. When organizations see that their investments generate positive results, they're more likely to fund similar projects in the future.

This realization changed how I viewed other grant consultants and successful entrepreneurs. Instead of seeing them as competition, I began viewing them as proof of what was possible.

I started celebrating others' success instead of feeling threatened by it. I began sharing resources and information freely instead of hoarding knowledge. I looked for ways to collaborate instead of always trying to compete.

This shift created a network effect that brought me more opportunities than I ever could have generated through competition alone.

THE REJECTION REFRAME

From a scarcity mindset, every grant rejection felt like personal failure and proof that I wasn't worthy of funding.

From an abundance mindset, rejections became information. They told me either that I hadn't found the right funder for my project or that I needed to improve my positioning and application quality.

This reframe was crucial because grant applications have high rejection rates. Even successful grant writers are turned down more often than they're approved. If you can't handle rejection without taking it personally, you won't persist long enough to achieve success.

I started viewing grant applications like sales calls: you expect some percentage to result in "no," but that doesn't mean you stop making calls. You just need to make enough quality applications to generate the approvals you need.

THE VALUE CREATION FOCUS

Perhaps the most important aspect of abundance thinking is the shift from "What can I get?" to "What can I give?"

Scarcity-minded grant applications focus on what the applicant needs:

- Money to pay bills
- Funding to start a business
- Capital to avoid bankruptcy
- Resources to solve personal problems

Abundance-minded grant applications focus on what the applicant will create:

- Jobs for community members
- Services for underserved populations
- Solutions to pressing social problems
- Educational opportunities for young people
- Economic development in distressed areas

Funders are looking for partners who can help them achieve their missions. They want to invest in value creators, not value extractors.

THE STRATEGIC APPROACH

Abundance thinking also leads to more strategic behavior.

Instead of applying for every grant you can find, you become selective about opportunities that align with your vision and values.

Instead of writing applications focused on immediate needs, you develop longer-term funding strategies.

Instead of treating each grant as an isolated opportunity, you begin building relationships with funders who could support multiple projects over time.

Instead of seeing grants as quick fixes, you view them as stepping stones toward larger goals.

This strategic approach leads to better outcomes and more sustainable funding relationships.

THE AUTHENTICITY BALANCE

One concern people sometimes have about shifting from scarcity to abundance positioning is whether it means being dishonest about their challenges.

The key is understanding the difference between authenticity and strategy.

You can be completely honest about your situation while choosing to emphasize different aspects of it. If your business is struggling, you don't have to hide that fact. But you can choose to focus on what you're doing to address the challenges rather than just describing the problems.

If you're facing financial difficulties, you can acknowledge that while emphasizing the opportunities that funding would create rather than the disasters it would prevent.

Abundance positioning isn't about fake positivity or denying reality— it's about choosing to lead with your vision rather than your problems.

THE RIPPLE EFFECTS

The mindset shift from scarcity to abundance affected every aspect of my business and personal life.

Client Relationships: I started attracting clients who were excited about growth rather than just desperate for survival. Working with vision-oriented people is more energizing and leads to better results.

Business Partnerships: Other professionals wanted to collaborate with someone who was building something meaningful rather than just trying to solve personal problems.

Personal Confidence: When you view yourself as a value creator rather than a charity case, your confidence naturally increases. This confidence shows up in how you present yourself, how you communicate, and how you make decisions.

Family Dynamics: My daughter began seeing entrepreneurship as something exciting and empowering rather than something stressful and overwhelming.

Financial Results: Abundance thinking led to better grant applications, which led to more funding approvals, which led to business growth, which led to personal financial stability.

THE TEACHING MOMENTS

As my coaching practice grew, I found myself constantly helping clients make this mindset shift. Here are some of the most common teaching moments:

From "I need money" to "I create value": Help clients articulate the specific value their business creates for customers, employees, and communities.

From "Times are tough" to "Opportunity exists": Guide clients to identify opportunities within their challenges and market gaps they're positioned to fill.

From "I deserve funding" to "I've earned investment": Show clients how to demonstrate their readiness for funding through past performance, clear planning, and strategic thinking.

From "Help me survive" to "Partner with my success": Teach clients to position funding as partnership opportunities rather than rescue missions.

THE COMPOUND EFFECTS

The beautiful thing about abundance thinking is that it creates compound effects over time.

When you consistently show up from abundance rather than scarcity, you build a reputation as someone who creates value and generates results. This reputation leads to more opportunities, better relationships, and increased resources.

When funders see that their investments in you generate positive outcomes, they're more likely to fund future projects and recommend you to other funding sources.

When other entrepreneurs see you as a value creator rather than a competitor, they're more likely to refer opportunities and collaborate on projects.

When potential clients see you as someone who helps others succeed rather than someone who's struggling to survive, they're more attracted to your services.

These compound effects can transform not just your financial situation, but your entire trajectory as an entrepreneur.

THE DAILY PRACTICE

Shifting from scarcity to abundance isn't a one-time decision—it's a daily practice that requires conscious effort until it becomes automatic.

Morning Intention: Start each day by focusing on what you're going to create rather than what you need to solve.

Language Awareness: Pay attention to how you describe your business, your challenges, and your goals. Are you leading with problems or possibilities?

Opportunity Recognition: Train yourself to see opportunities within challenges rather than just obstacles.

Value Articulation: Practice describing the value you create in clear, compelling terms.

Success Celebration: Acknowledge and celebrate progress, even small wins, rather than only focusing on what's still not working.

Gratitude Practice: Regularly recognize and appreciate the resources, relationships, and opportunities you already have.

YOUR ABUNDANCE TRANSFORMATION

As you consider your own mindset and how it affects your approach to funding and business building, ask yourself these questions:

When you describe your business to others, do you lead with problems or possibilities?

When you think about applying for grants, are you focused on what you need or what you can create?

When you face challenges, do you see them as evidence of failure or information about what to adjust?

When others succeed in your industry, do you feel threatened or inspired?

When you communicate with potential funders, partners, or clients, are you positioning yourself as someone who needs rescue or someone who creates value?

The answers to these questions will reveal whether you're operating from scarcity or abundance, and they'll predict your likely success with grants and other funding opportunities.

In the next chapter, we'll explore how the Coach K philosophy developed and how building a brand around education and empowerment became the foundation for sustainable business success.

But for now, remember this: Funders don't invest in problems—they invest in solutions. They don't partner with victims—they partner with value creators. They don't rescue struggling businesses—they amplify successful ones.

Your mindset determines which category you fall into. Choose abundance.

CHAPTER 8

THE COACH K PHILOSOPHY

"**Y**ou couldn't pay me to do it. I'll never coach. These are things I'm actively saying, like, never."

That's what I told my friend Mel Bowers when she suggested I should start teaching people about grants and business funding. I was adamant—absolutely certain—that coaching wasn't for me.

Famous last words, right?

Fast forward a few years, and "Coach K" has become not just my professional identity, but my mission, my passion, and the vehicle through which I'm changing lives and democratizing access to capital. The journey from "I'll never coach" to building a coaching empire taught me everything about authentic brand building, the power of education over extraction, and what it really means to create legacy.

Let me tell you how someone who swore she'd never coach became known as The Grant Expert™, and more importantly, how the philosophy behind that transformation can guide your own path to meaningful success.

THE RELUCTANT BEGINNING

When I first started having success with grants, people began asking questions. It started innocently enough—friends, former colleagues, people in my network who saw my social media posts about grant wins.

"How did you find that grant?" "What did you write in your application?" "Do you think I could qualify for something like that?"

I was happy to help, answering questions when they came up, sharing resources when I found them. But I had no intention of making it a business. I was still focused on my own grant applications and trying to grow my funding consulting practice.

But the questions kept coming. And they became more frequent. And more detailed.

People weren't just curious—they were hungry for this information. They had been operating under the same false assumptions I had held about grants being only for nonprofits or requiring expensive grant writers. They wanted to learn how to access this funding themselves.

That's when Mel suggested I should start formally teaching what I was learning.

"People need to hear from you," she said. "They need to know how you're doing all of these amazing things."

My response was immediate and definitive: "Nope, absolutely not. I'm not gonna do it. I'll never coach. You couldn't pay me to do it."

THE MINDSET BEHIND THE RESISTANCE

Why was I so resistant to coaching? Several reasons, really.

First, I was still working through my own challenges. My business was growing but not yet stable. I was learning the grant system myself and didn't feel qualified to teach others. Who was I to position myself as an expert when I was still figuring things out?

Second, I had seen too many people in the entrepreneurship space who seemed more focused on selling courses than actually helping people succeed. I didn't want to be associated with that kind of predatory education market.

Third, I was an introvert at heart. Despite my success in banking and networking, I preferred working behind the scenes to being front and center. The idea of putting myself out there as a teacher or speaker felt uncomfortable and inauthentic.

But most importantly, I believed that the best way to help people was to do the work for them, not to teach them how to do it themselves. I thought grant writing services would be more valuable than grant education.

I was wrong about that last part.

THE MIAMI MOMENT

The turning point came during a girls' trip to Miami. We were out to dinner, and I was in a good mood—good enough to pick up the entire tab for the table. As I was paying, I jokingly said, "Anybody want to ask me a business question so I can make this a tax write-off?"

I was laughing, but someone actually asked a question. Then someone else asked another. And before I knew it, we were having a two-hour conversation about business, grants, and entrepreneurship.

What surprised me wasn't that the conversation went long—it was that my close friends, people I thought I knew well, were genuinely interested in becoming entrepreneurs. They had questions about business structure, funding, marketing, all the things I had been learning through my own journey.

"You should coach," one of them said. "You should start teaching this information."

Others chimed in: "You should get on social media." "People need to hear this." "You're really good at explaining things."

I was still resistant, but something had shifted. I realized that even the people closest to me wanted this information, and if they needed it, probably a lot of other people did too.

THE TESTING PHASE

Even after the Miami conversation, I wasn't ready to launch a full coaching business. Instead, I decided to test the waters with a very low-risk approach.

I had an empty rental property in Nashville, so I decided to host a free workshop there. I'd invite anyone who wanted to learn about grants to come, and I'd share what I knew. No charge, no pressure, just information sharing.

I figured maybe a dozen people would show up.

The room was packed wall to wall.

People were sitting on the floor, leaning against walls, taking notes furiously. The energy in the room was electric—people were hungry for this information and grateful that someone was sharing it freely.

After the Nashville event, people in Huntsville started asking, "What about us?" So I hosted another free workshop in Huntsville.

Same result—wall to wall attendance, engaged participants, grateful feedback.

That's when I knew I had stumbled onto something significant.

THE PHILOSOPHY EMERGES

Through those early workshops and the individual coaching that followed, I began developing what would become the Coach K philosophy. It wasn't a planned brand strategy—it was an organic response to what I saw people needed most.

Education Over Exploitation: Instead of charging thousands to write grants for people, I would teach them how to write grants themselves. This approach was more sustainable, more empowering, and created better long-term results.

Accessibility Over Exclusivity: Grant funding shouldn't be limited to people with expensive consultants or insider connections. Anyone should be able to learn these skills and access these opportunities.

Community Over Competition: Rather than hoarding information, I would share it freely, knowing that everyone's success creates more opportunities for everyone else.

Empowerment Over Dependency: My goal wasn't to create clients who needed me forever, but to create entrepreneurs who could succeed independently.

Results Over Rhetoric: Everything I taught had to be based on real results, not just theory or inspiration.

This philosophy differentiated me from other people in the grant consulting space and established the foundation for everything that followed.

THE EDUCATOR VERSUS GRANT WRITER DECISION

One of the most important decisions I made was choosing to position myself as an educator rather than a grant writer.

Traditional grant writers charge between $5,000 and $10,000 per application, with no guarantee of success. Even if they have high success rates, most small business owners can't afford those fees, especially when they're already struggling financially.

I realized I could have much more impact by teaching people how to write their own grants. For a fraction of the cost of hiring a grant writer, entrepreneurs could learn skills that would serve them for years and help them secure multiple funding opportunities.

This decision was partly philosophical—I believe in empowering people with knowledge rather than creating dependence—and partly practical. I could help far more people this way, and the economics worked better for everyone involved.

It also set me apart in the marketplace. While other consultants were competing on who could write the best applications, I was focused on who could provide the best education.

THE NAME THAT STUCK

"Coach K" wasn't a planned brand name—it evolved naturally from people not being able to pronounce "Jekwenta."

Throughout my life, people have struggled with my name. At Wells Fargo, customers would come in asking for "the K girl" when they couldn't remember how to say it. Family and friends have always called me "Quinn" or "Quina" for simplicity.

But when I started helping people with business questions, "Coach K" emerged organically. People would see me in public and say, "Hey, Coach K, I have a question for you."

The name felt right because it captured what I was becoming: someone who guided others toward their goals rather than doing the work for them. It implied partnership and empowerment rather than dependency.

As the brand grew, "Coach K" became synonymous with accessible grant education and practical business guidance. It represented someone who had been where my clients were and could show them the way forward.

THE BRICK-BY-BRICK APPROACH

One thing I'm most proud of about the Coach K brand is that it was built organically, brick by brick, based on real results and genuine relationships.

I didn't start with a massive marketing budget or elaborate launch strategy. I started by helping one person at a time, hosting free workshops, sharing valuable information on social media, and consistently showing up for my community.

Each client success story became proof of concept. Each workshop attendee became a potential referral source. Each social media post sharing real results became evidence that my approach worked.

This organic growth approach took longer than some other strategies might have, but it created a solid foundation of credibility and trust that has sustained long-term success.

THE HEART OF THE BRAND

At its core, the Coach K brand represents something specific: democratizing access to funding and financial education.

I saw too many people trapped by lack of information—people taking out predatory loans because they didn't know about grants, people giving up on business dreams because they couldn't access traditional funding, people staying in corporate jobs they hated because they didn't know how to fund their entrepreneurial ambitions.

The Coach K mission became about changing that narrative. About showing people that funding opportunities exist specifically for them. About proving that you don't need special connections or expensive consultants to access capital. About demonstrating that financial education is the key to breaking cycles of dependence and building generational wealth.

This mission gives everything I do deeper meaning beyond just business success.

THE TEACHING METHODOLOGY

As my coaching practice grew, I refined my teaching methodology based on what actually helped people achieve results.

Start with Mindset: Before diving into tactical applications, I help people shift from scarcity to abundance thinking. This foundational work makes everything else more effective.

Focus on Systems: Rather than just providing information, I help people build systems for finding grants, organizing applications, and tracking results.

Emphasize Implementation: Knowledge without action is worthless. My programs are designed to push people toward taking concrete steps, not just consuming information.

Provide Ongoing Support: Learning to write grants is a skill that develops over time. I create communities and resources that support people through their entire journey.

Celebrate Wins: Every grant approval, no matter how small, gets celebrated. This builds momentum and encourages persistence.

Learn from Losses: Rejections become learning opportunities. We analyze what didn't work and adjust the approach for next time.

This methodology produces consistent results because it addresses both the technical and psychological aspects of grant success.

THE RIPPLE EFFECT

What I discovered as Coach K grew was that helping people access grants creates ripple effects that extend far beyond individual funding approvals.

When someone uses grants to start or grow a business, they often create jobs for other people. When they succeed, they become examples for their communities about what's possible. When they learn these skills, they often teach family members and friends.

Kathy, who secured $40,000 in her first few months, went on to help other women in her network apply for grants. Emma, who has received nearly a million dollars in funding, has become a mentor for entrepreneurs in her community. Megan, with her $2.6 million in funding across multiple organizations, has created dozens of jobs and serves hundreds of families.

This multiplier effect means that every person I teach potentially impacts many others. It's why the education model is so much more powerful than the service model.

THE CREDIBILITY BUILDING

Building credibility as Coach K required consistently delivering results and being transparent about both successes and failures.

I shared real numbers—specific grant amounts, actual timelines, honest success rates. I showcased client wins while also discussing applications that didn't work and lessons learned from rejections.

I was careful not to overpromise or create unrealistic expectations. Grant success requires work, persistence, and often multiple attempts. I made sure people understood this going in.

I also continued applying for grants myself, staying current with changes in the funding landscape and maintaining my own track record of success. You can't teach what you don't practice.

This commitment to authenticity and transparency built trust that has sustained the brand through various market changes and competitive pressures.

THE LEGACY VISION

As Coach K evolved from accidental brand to intentional mission, I began thinking more strategically about legacy and long-term impact.

My goal became to create the "Earn Your Leisure of grants"—to be the go-to resource for grant education the way Troy Millings and Rashad Bilal became the go-to resource for financial education in the Black community.

This vision means building something that transcends my individual coaching and creates systemic change in how people access capital and think about funding.

It means training other coaches who can carry this message to different communities and industries. It means creating resources that can help people even when they can't work with me directly. It means influencing policy and funding practices to be more accessible and equitable.

THE AUTHENTICATION PROCESS

One challenge of building a personal brand around expertise is constantly having to prove your credibility, especially as a Black woman in business and finance.

I've had to be very intentional about documenting results, sharing specific examples, and letting client success stories speak for themselves. I've had to balance confidence with humility, authority with accessibility.

The authentication process has been ongoing—every speaking engagement, every media appearance, every client success adds to the credibility bank account. But it requires consistent effort and vigilance to maintain.

THE EVOLUTION CONTINUES

The beautiful thing about the Coach K brand is that it continues evolving as I grow and learn. What started as grant education has expanded to include broader business funding strategies, entrepreneurship mindset work, and wealth-building education.

The core mission remains the same—democratizing access to capital and financial education—but the methods and reach continue expanding.

This evolution keeps the work fresh and meaningful while allowing me to serve people at different stages of their entrepreneurial journeys.

YOUR BRAND PHILOSOPHY

As you think about building your own brand and business, consider these questions:

What expertise do you have that others need?

How can you serve people in a way that empowers rather than creates dependence?

What mission or cause gives your work deeper meaning beyond just making money?

How can you build credibility organically through real results rather than just marketing?

What legacy do you want to create through your business?

Your brand philosophy will guide every decision you make about how to position yourself, whom to serve, and how to create value. It will determine whether you build something sustainable and meaningful or just another transaction-based business.

In the next chapter, we'll dive into the specific grant strategies and methodologies that have helped my clients secure millions in funding. We'll start with the foundational work of debunking myths and preparing for grant success.

But remember this: Your brand isn't what you say about yourself—it's what others experience when they interact with you. Make sure every touchpoint reinforces the values and mission you want to be known for.

That's the Coach K philosophy. That's how you build something that matters.

CHAPTER 9

GRANT MYTHS DEBUNKED

"I thought grants were only for nonprofits."

I hear this statement at least once a week from entrepreneurs who have been operating under false assumptions about grant funding. And honestly, I understand why they think this—I believed the same myths for years.

These misconceptions aren't just innocent mistakes. They're barriers that keep thousands of qualified business owners from accessing funding that could transform their companies and their lives. They're the reason many entrepreneurs struggle with traditional funding when grant opportunities are sitting right there, waiting for someone to apply.

Before we dive into the practical aspects of finding and winning grants, we need to clear the air about what grants actually are, who can get them, and how the process really works. Because if you're operating from false assumptions, even the best strategies won't help you succeed.

Let me walk you through the biggest myths that keep people from even trying—and show you the reality that could change everything for your business.

MYTH #1: "YOU HAVE TO BE A NONPROFIT TO GET GRANTS"

This is the granddaddy of all grant myths, and it's probably cost more entrepreneurs more money than any other misconception.

The Myth: Only nonprofit organizations qualify for grant funding. For-profit businesses need to stick to loans, investors, or self-funding.

The Reality: There are thousands of grants specifically designed for for-profit businesses. In fact, many funders prefer working with for-profit entities because they tend to be more sustainable and results-oriented than nonprofits.

Here's where this myth comes from: Many government grants and foundation grants are indeed designated for nonprofits. When people research grants, these are often the first ones they find, leading them to assume all grants work this way.

But here's what they're missing: Corporate foundations, economic development organizations, industry associations, and even some government programs specifically fund for-profit businesses that align with their goals.

I've personally helped for-profit businesses secure grants from:

- Corporate foundations that want to support small business development
- Economic development agencies that fund job creation
- Industry associations that support innovation and growth
- Government programs designed to stimulate specific sectors

The key is understanding that funders don't care about your tax status as much as they care about your mission alignment and potential impact.

MYTH #2: "YOU NEED TO HIRE A GRANT WRITER"

This myth is particularly damaging because it creates an unnecessary financial barrier for many entrepreneurs.

The Myth: Grant applications are so complex that you need to hire a professional grant writer who charges $5,000-$10,000 per application.

The Reality: While grant writers can be helpful, they're not necessary for success. Many of my most successful clients have written their own applications and secured hundreds of thousands or even millions in funding.

Here's the truth about grant writers:

- They typically charge $5,000-$10,000 per application
- They cannot guarantee approval
- They often know less about your business than you do
- They may not understand your industry or community context
- They're working on multiple applications simultaneously, so you're not their only priority

Compare this to learning to write grants yourself:

- You understand your business better than anyone else
- You can write multiple applications for the cost of one grant writer
- You can apply for grants whenever you find opportunities
- You build a valuable skill that serves you for years

- You can adjust your approach based on feedback and results

The most successful grant applicants I know write their own applications because they can communicate their vision and passion in ways that no hired writer ever could.

MYTH #3: "GRANTS ARE JUST FREE MONEY"

This myth is dangerous because it creates the wrong expectations and approach.

The Myth: Grants are just free money that you can use however you want, like winning the lottery.

The Reality: Grants are strategic investments made by organizations that want to achieve specific outcomes. They come with expectations, reporting requirements, and accountability measures.

When you receive a grant, you're entering into a partnership with the funder. They expect you to:

- Use the money for the purposes outlined in your application
- Achieve the results you promised
- Report on your progress and outcomes
- Represent their investment well
- Sometimes provide recognition or marketing benefits

This isn't a burden—it's actually what makes grants powerful. Because funders want you to succeed, they often provide additional support beyond money, including:

- Mentorship and guidance
- Networking opportunities
- Marketing and publicity
- Access to other resources
- Introductions to potential partners or customers

Understanding this partnership mindset is crucial for both winning grants and succeeding after you receive them.

MYTH #4: "YOU HAVE TO PAY GRANTS BACK"

This myth often comes from confusion between grants and loans.

The Myth: All business funding has to be repaid with interest.

The Reality: True grants never have to be repaid. That's what makes them different from loans, lines of credit, or investor funding.

However, there are some important nuances:

- If you don't fulfill the terms of your grant agreement, you might have to return the money
- Some programs call themselves "grants" but are actually forgivable loans with specific conditions
- You need to read grant terms carefully to understand any requirements or restrictions

But legitimate grants—funding provided by foundations, corporations, or government agencies to support projects that align with their missions—do not require repayment.

This is why grants are such powerful funding tools: they provide capital without creating debt or requiring you to give up equity in your business.

MYTH #5: "THE COMPETITION IS TOO FIERCE"

This myth stops people from even trying.

The Myth: So many people apply for grants that small businesses don't have a realistic chance of winning.

The Reality: While grants are competitive, most people never apply because they believe myths like the ones we're debunking right now.

Here's what's actually happening:

- Many grant opportunities receive fewer applications than you might expect
- Most applications are poorly written or don't follow guidelines
- Many applicants don't position themselves effectively
- Some grants go unused because organizations can't find qualified applicants

Your real competition isn't thousands of applicants—it's the few who apply properly, follow guidelines, and position their projects effectively.

I've seen grants with application periods that get extended because they didn't receive enough qualified submissions. I've worked with clients who won grants on their first try because they followed basic guidelines that many other applicants ignored.

The competition is fierce among people who don't know what they're doing. Among people who understand grant strategy and positioning, the odds are much better.

MYTH #6: "YOU NEED SPECIAL CONNECTIONS OR INSIDER ACCESS"

This myth particularly affects minority entrepreneurs and women business owners.

The Myth: Grant funding is controlled by an "old boys' network" that only funds people with special connections.

The Reality: While relationships can be helpful, most grants are awarded based on how well applications meet the funder's criteria and goals.

The best way to build relationships with funders is to:

- Research their mission and priorities
- Apply for grants that genuinely align with your work
- Follow their guidelines precisely
- Deliver on your promises when you receive funding
- Report your results and impact clearly

Many of my most successful clients started with no connections in the grant world. They built relationships by being professional, reliable, and results-oriented.

MYTH #7: "GRANTS ARE ONLY FOR CERTAIN TYPES OF BUSINESSES"

This myth limits people's thinking about what qualifies for funding.

The Myth: Only businesses in specific industries like nonprofits, healthcare, or education can get grants.

The Reality: Grants exist for virtually every type of business, depending on how you position your work and which funders you target.

I've helped secure grants for:

- Childcare centers
- Food trucks
- Tech startups
- Manufacturing companies
- Retail businesses
- Service providers
- Creative enterprises
- And many others

The key is understanding that funders care more about impact than industry. If your business creates jobs, serves underserved communities, solves social problems, promotes economic development, or advances innovation, there are likely grants available for you.

MYTH #8: "YOU NEED TO BE STRUGGLING TO QUALIFY"

This myth comes from confusion about the purpose of grants.

The Myth: Grants are designed to rescue failing businesses or help people in desperate situations.

The Reality: Most funders prefer to invest in businesses that are already showing signs of success and have clear plans for growth and impact.

Funders want to amplify success, not rescue failure. They're looking for:

- Businesses with clear vision and strategy
- Entrepreneurs who have demonstrated capability
- Projects with realistic timelines and budgets
- Organizations that can deliver measurable results

This doesn't mean you need to be wildly successful to qualify for grants. But it does mean you need to position yourself as someone who can effectively use funding to create positive outcomes.

MYTH #9: "GRANT APPLICATIONS ARE INCREDIBLY COMPLEX"

This myth intimidates people before they even start.

The Myth: Grant applications require advanced degrees, complex financial projections, and hundreds of pages of documentation.

The Reality: Many successful grant applications are relatively straight-forward documents that clearly explain what you want to do and why it matters.

The most effective grant applications focus on:

- Clear problem identification
- Compelling solution description
- Realistic budget and timeline
- Measurable outcomes and impact
- Strong organizational capacity

You don't need an MBA or advanced writing skills. You need clarity about your project and the ability to communicate why it deserves funding.

MYTH #10: "IF YOU GET REJECTED ONCE, YOU SHOULDN'T APPLY AGAIN"

This myth prevents people from building the persistence necessary for grant success.

The Myth: Rejection means you don't qualify and shouldn't waste time applying to that funder again.

The Reality: Rejection often means your timing wasn't right, your positioning needed improvement, or the funder had different priorities that funding cycle.

Many successful grant recipients were rejected multiple times before winning funding. Rejection can provide valuable feedback about how to improve your applications.

Some funders explicitly encourage reapplication after you've addressed feedback from previous submissions. Others have annual funding cycles where priorities and available money change from year to year.

Persistence, combined with continuous improvement, is often the difference between grant success and failure.

THE TRUTH ABOUT GRANT SUCCESS

Now that we've cleared up these myths, here's what grant success actually requires:

Research: Finding grants that align with your business and mission.

Positioning: Presenting your business as a solution to problems funders care about.

Strategy: Understanding what funders want and how to give it to them.

Persistence: Continuing to apply even when you face rejections.

Professional Execution: Following guidelines, meeting deadlines, and communicating clearly.

Results Delivery: Doing what you promised and reporting your impact.

None of these requirements are insurmountable. They're all skills you can learn and improve over time.

THE COST OF BELIEVING MYTHS

Before we move forward, I want you to consider what these myths might have cost you already.

How many grant opportunities have you ignored because you assumed you didn't qualify?

How much money have you borrowed at high interest rates when grant funding might have been available?

How many business ideas have you shelved because you couldn't access traditional funding and didn't know about grants?

How much stress and financial pressure have you endured while grant opportunities sat undiscovered?

The cost of believing myths about grants isn't just missed opportunities—it's the compound effect of making business decisions based on incomplete information.

THE OPPORTUNITY AHEAD

Here's the exciting truth: most of your competition is still operating under these same myths. While they're assuming they don't qualify, you can be researching opportunities. While they're believing grants are too complicated, you can be learning the system. While they're convinced the competition is too fierce, you can be submitting strong applications to grants that receive fewer submissions than you'd expect.

The grant landscape is more accessible than most people realize, and that creates opportunity for entrepreneurs who are willing to learn the reality behind the myths.

YOUR MYTH AUDIT

Before moving to the next chapter, take an honest inventory of which myths you might have been believing:

☐ Did you assume grants were only for nonprofits? ☐ Have you avoided applying because you thought you needed to hire an expensive grant writer? ☐ Did you think grants were just free money with no strings attached? ☐ Were you confused about whether grants need to be repaid? ☐ Have you been intimidated by what you assumed was fierce competition? ☐ Did you think you needed special connections to access funding? ☐ Have you limited your thinking about what types of businesses qualify? ☐ Did you assume you needed to be struggling to get grants? ☐ Were you intimidated by the perceived complexity of applications? ☐ Have you given up too easily after early rejections?

Identifying which myths have been limiting your thinking is the first step toward accessing the funding opportunities that have been available all along.

In the next chapter, we'll explore exactly who qualifies for grants and how to identify the opportunities that are the best fit for your specific business and situation. You might be surprised by how many funding sources are designed for businesses exactly like yours.

But for now, let me leave you with this: The biggest barriers to grant success aren't in the system—they're in our assumptions about the system. Now that you know the truth, you can start taking action based on reality instead of myths.

The funding is out there. The question is: Are you ready to go get it?

CHAPTER 10

THE FOUNDATION FOR SUCCESS

"Everyone qualifies for a grant. It's all about how you position your business and what you aim to do with the funding that opens up the door for you to get access to funding."

This statement surprises people every time I say it. But it's absolutely true. The question isn't whether you qualify for grants—it's whether you've positioned yourself and your business to take advantage of the opportunities that exist.

Think of grant readiness like preparing for a job interview. You might be the perfect candidate, but if you show up without a resume, wearing inappropriate clothes, and unable to articulate your value, you're not going to get the position. The same principle applies to grants: you need the right foundation in place before you can successfully compete for funding.

In this chapter, I'm going to walk you through exactly what that foundation looks like and how to build it, even if you're just getting started with your business idea.

THE BUSINESS STRUCTURE FOUNDATION

The very first element of grant readiness is having your business properly structured as a legal entity. This is non-negotiable, and it's something you need to do even if you're still in the planning stages of your business.

Why Legal Structure Matters

When funders evaluate grant applications, they're assessing risk. An unregistered business idea represents higher risk than a legally established entity with proper documentation. Even if you haven't started generating revenue yet, having that legal structure signals that you're serious about your business and committed to operating professionally.

More importantly, different types of funding opportunities become available based on your business structure. While there are some grants for individuals with business ideas, there's an ocean of opportunities for legally established entities.

Your Structure Options

- **LLC (Limited Liability Company)**: Most flexible option for small businesses, provides liability protection, and is recognized by most funders
- **Corporation (C-Corp or S-Corp)**: More complex but sometimes required for certain types of grants, especially larger amounts
- **Nonprofit Organization**: Required for grants specifically designated for nonprofits, but limits your business model options

For most entrepreneurs, an LLC is the best starting point. It's relatively inexpensive to establish, provides legal protection, and qualifies you for the vast majority of business grants.

When to Register

Here's my advice: register your business as soon as you have a clear idea of what you want to do, even if you haven't started operations yet. Don't wait until you're "ready" or have everything figured out. The legal structure is a foundation that enables everything else.

I've seen too many entrepreneurs miss grant opportunities because they were still operating as sole proprietors or hadn't formalized their business structure. Don't let bureaucratic delays cost you funding opportunities.

THE FEDERAL IDENTIFICATION REQUIREMENTS

Once you have your legal structure, you need proper identification numbers from the IRS and other agencies.

Employer Identification Number (EIN)

Every business needs an EIN, also called a Federal Tax ID number. This is free to obtain directly from the IRS and is required for:

- Opening business bank accounts
- Applying for most grants
- Filing business tax returns
- Hiring employees
- Many other business activities

Getting your EIN is straightforward and can be done online at the IRS website. Beware of companies that charge fees for this service—it's free when you go directly through the IRS.

DUNS Number

Many federal grants and some private grants require a DUNS (Data Universal Numbering System) number, which is a unique identifier for your business. This is also free to obtain through Dun & Bradstreet.

SAM Registration

If you plan to apply for federal grants, you'll need to register in the System for Award Management (SAM). This is a more complex process that can take several weeks, so start early if federal funding is part of your strategy.

THE BUSINESS ADDRESS REQUIREMENT

You need a legitimate business address that's not your home address. This doesn't mean you need to rent expensive office space—there are several options:

Virtual Office Services: These provide a professional business address and often include mail forwarding services. Costs typically range from $20-100 per month.

Shared Office Spaces: Co-working facilities often allow you to use their address for business purposes.

Commercial Mail Boxes: Some postal services and shipping stores offer business address services.

Family or Friend's Business: If someone you trust has a business address, they might allow you to use it temporarily.

The key is having an address that looks professional and can receive business mail reliably. Many funders will send materials to your business address, and having mail returned can negatively impact your application.

THE DIGITAL PRESENCE FOUNDATION

In today's world, your digital presence is often the first impression funders have of your business. This "brand appearance" needs to communicate professionalism and credibility.

Business Website

You don't need an expensive, complex website, but you do need something that clearly communicates:

- What your business does
- Who you serve
- How to contact you
- Your professional background and qualifications

A simple, clean website built on platforms like WordPress, Squarespace, or Wix can be created for under $200 and will serve you well for grant applications.

Business Email Address

Nothing says "amateur" like applying for a grant from a Gmail or Yahoo email address. Get a professional email address that matches your domain name (like Jekwenta@coachkprimm.com instead of Jekwentaprimm@ gmail.com).

This is usually included with website hosting and costs just a few dollars per month.

Social Media Presence

You don't need to be on every platform, but you should have professional profiles on:

- LinkedIn (essential for business credibility)
- Facebook (business page, not personal profile)
- Instagram (if relevant to your industry)

Keep these profiles updated, professional, and aligned with your business messaging. Funders often check social media to get a sense of your business and character.

THE FINANCIAL FOUNDATION

Even if your business isn't generating revenue yet, you need proper financial systems in place.

Business Bank Account

Separate your business and personal finances immediately. This serves multiple purposes:

- Demonstrates professional financial management
- Makes grant reporting much easier

- Provides legal protection for your personal assets
- Shows funders that you understand basic business principles

Most banks require an EIN and business registration documents to open a business account.

Basic Accounting System

You don't need expensive software, but you do need a system for tracking:

- Income and expenses
- Financial projections
- Budget management

Simple options include QuickBooks, FreshBooks, or even well-organized spreadsheets. The key is having organized financial information readily available for grant applications.

Financial Projections

Most grant applications ask for budget information and financial projections. Even if your business is new, you should have:

- Realistic revenue projections
- Detailed expense budgets
- Clear financial goals
- Understanding of your funding needs

THE PROBLEM-SOLUTION FRAMEWORK

This is where many entrepreneurs struggle, but it's absolutely crucial for grant success. You need to clearly articulate:

The Problem You're Solving

Great entrepreneurs solve problems. Grant funders invest in solutions to problems they care about. You need to identify and clearly describe:

- A specific problem in your community or industry
- Who is affected by this problem
- Why current solutions are inadequate
- The cost or impact of leaving this problem unsolved

Your Solution

Your business should be positioned as the solution to the problem you've identified. This means clearly explaining:

- How your product or service addresses the problem
- Why your approach is better than existing alternatives
- What makes you qualified to implement this solution
- How you'll measure success

The Impact Potential

Funders want to see that their investment will create meaningful impact. You should be able to articulate:

- How many people will benefit from your solution
- What specific outcomes you'll achieve

- How success will be measured and reported
- The long-term sustainability of your solution

THE DOCUMENTATION SYSTEM

Organization is crucial for grant success. You need systems for managing:

Document Storage

Create organized folders (digital and physical) for:

- Business registration documents
- Financial records
- Grant applications and submissions
- Correspondence with funders
- Marketing materials and press coverage

Application Tracking

Develop a system for tracking:

- Grant opportunities you've identified
- Application deadlines and requirements
- Submission status and follow-up needs
- Results and feedback received

Contact Management

Keep organized records of:

- Funder contact information
- Previous communications

- Relationship notes and preferences
- Networking contacts and referrals

THE CREDIBILITY BUILDING

Even new businesses can build credibility through:

Professional Development

- Industry certifications or training
- Business education or workshops
- Networking event participation
- Professional association memberships

Community Involvement

- Volunteer work related to your business mission
- Speaking at local events
- Participation in community organizations
- Media coverage or publicity

Strategic Partnerships

- Relationships with established businesses
- Mentorship from successful entrepreneurs
- Advisory board members
- Professional service providers (attorney, accountant, etc.)

THE TIMELINE FOR BUILDING YOUR FOUNDATION

Many entrepreneurs ask how long it takes to get "grant ready." Here's a realistic timeline:

Week 1-2: Business registration and EIN application **Week 3-4**: Business address and bank account setup **Week 5-6**: Basic website and email setup **Week 7-8**: Social media profiles and financial systems **Week 9-10**: Documentation organization and initial grant research

This timeline assumes you're working on foundation building part-time while managing other responsibilities. If you can dedicate more time, the process can be accelerated.

The key is not to wait until everything is perfect. Once you have the basics in place, you can start applying for grants while continuing to strengthen your foundation.

THE INVESTMENT REQUIRED

Building a proper foundation requires some upfront investment, but it's much less than most people expect:

- Business registration: $50-500 (varies by state)
- EIN: Free (from IRS directly)
- Business address: $20-100/month
- Basic website: $100-300 initially, $10-30/month ongoing
- Business email: $5-15/month
- Bank account: Usually free with minimum balance
- Basic accounting software: $10-50/month

Total initial investment: $500-1,500 Monthly ongoing costs: $50-200

This investment pays for itself with your first grant approval. And remember, these are legitimate business expenses that are tax-deductible.

THE MINDSET COMPONENT

Building your foundation isn't just about paperwork and systems—it's about stepping into your identity as a business owner and grant recipient.

Many entrepreneurs struggle with imposter syndrome during this phase. They feel like they're "playing business" or that they don't deserve professional systems and processes.

Here's the truth: you deserve professional systems because you're a professional entrepreneur. You deserve to compete for grants because you have valuable solutions to offer. You deserve success because you're willing to do the work required to achieve it.

Building your foundation is an act of faith in your own potential and commitment to your business success.

THE COMMON MISTAKES TO AVOID

Waiting for Perfect Timing: Don't wait until your business is fully developed to build your foundation. Start where you are and improve as you go.

Cutting Corners on Professionalism: Cheap shortcuts often cost more in the long run. Invest in doing things right from the beginning.

Inconsistent Information: Make sure all your business information is consistent across all platforms and documents.

Ignoring Legal Requirements: Don't skip steps like business registration or proper licensing. Compliance issues can disqualify you from funding.

Poor Organization: Disorganized documentation will slow down your grant applications and may cost you opportunities.

YOUR FOUNDATION CHECKLIST

Before moving to the next chapter, make sure you have:

☐ Legal business structure (LLC, Corporation, etc.) ☐ Employer Identification Number (EIN) ☐ Legitimate business address ☐ Professional business email address ☐ Basic business website ☐ Business bank account ☐ LinkedIn business profile ☐ Basic accounting system ☐ Clear problem-solution positioning ☐ Document organization system ☐ Financial projections and budgets

If you're missing any of these elements, prioritize getting them in place before you start seriously pursuing grants. A strong foundation makes everything else easier and more effective.

In the next chapter, we'll dive into the strategy of finding grants that match your business and mission. But remember: strategy built on a weak foundation will always underperform. Take the time to build these systems properly, and they'll serve you throughout your entrepreneurial journey.

Your foundation isn't just about qualifying for grants—it's about building a business that's sustainable, professional, and positioned for long-term success. The grants are just the beginning.

CHAPTER 11

FINDING THE RIGHT GRANTS

"**P**eople put themselves in a bubble, so they look for industry specific grants. But when you put yourself in a bubble, you limit yourself on opportunities."

This is one of the biggest mistakes I see entrepreneurs make when they start their grant search. They think, "I'm starting a trucking business, so I need trucking grants," or "I'm opening a restaurant, so I need food service grants."

While industry-specific grants do exist, this narrow thinking causes people to miss thousands of opportunities that could fund their business based on the impact they create, the communities they serve, or the problems they solve.

The secret to successful grant finding isn't just knowing where to look— it's knowing how to think beyond your industry and position your business to qualify for funding sources you never would have considered.

Let me show you how to expand your search strategy and find grants that others in your industry are completely overlooking.

THE MINDSET SHIFT: FROM INDUSTRY TO IMPACT

When most people search for grants, they start with their business category. But successful grant seekers start with their impact.

Instead of asking "What grants exist for daycare centers?" I learned to ask "What grants exist for businesses that serve working families, create jobs, provide educational programming, or support economic development?"

This shift opened up funding categories I never would have found otherwise:

- Workforce development grants (because childcare enables parents to work)
- Economic development grants (because we created jobs in our community)
- Education grants (because we provided early childhood programming)
- Women's empowerment grants (because we supported working mothers)

Your business probably creates multiple types of impact. The key is identifying all of them and searching for grants that support each type of outcome.

THE IMPACT MAPPING EXERCISE

Before you start searching for grants, complete this impact mapping exercise:

Direct Impact: Who directly benefits from your product or service?

- Your immediate customers
- The people who use what you create
- The communities where you operate

Indirect Impact: Who benefits from the success of your direct customers?

- Family members of your customers
- Employers of your customers
- Other businesses in your ecosystem

Economic Impact: How does your business affect the local economy?

- Jobs you create
- Money you spend with local suppliers
- Taxes you pay
- Economic activity you generate

Social Impact: What social problems does your business help solve?

- Educational gaps you address
- Health issues you improve
- Environmental problems you reduce
- Social inequities you help overcome

Community Impact: How does your business strengthen communities?

- Services you provide that didn't exist before
- Community partnerships you create
- Local leadership you provide
- Positive examples you set

Each type of impact represents potential grant categories to explore.

THE FOUR MAIN CATEGORIES OF GRANT FUNDERS

Understanding the different types of organizations that provide grants helps you target your search more effectively.

1. Government Grants

Federal, state, and local government agencies provide grants to advance public policy goals:

Federal Grants:

- Small Business Administration (SBA)
- Department of Agriculture (USDA)
- Department of Commerce
- Department of Health and Human Services
- Department of Education
- Environmental Protection Agency (EPA)

State Grants:

- Economic development agencies
- Workforce development boards

- Tourism and agriculture departments
- Small business development centers

Local Grants:

- City economic development offices
- County business development programs
- Municipal revitalization initiatives
- Local tourism boards

Government grants often have specific geographic, demographic, or industry requirements, but they also tend to offer larger funding amounts.

2. Foundation Grants

Private foundations use grant funding to advance their charitable missions:

Corporate Foundations:

- Wells Fargo Foundation
- Bank of America Foundation
- Walmart Foundation
- FedEx Foundation
- Many others with missions related to small business, economic development, or community support

Family Foundations:

- Established by wealthy individuals or families
- Often focused on specific geographic areas or causes
- May have more flexible requirements than corporate foundations

Community Foundations:

- Serve specific geographic regions
- Pool donations from multiple sources
- Often prioritize local economic development and community improvement

Foundations typically have clear mission statements that tell you exactly what types of projects they want to fund.

3. Corporate Grants

Many corporations provide grants directly (not through foundations) as part of their:

- Corporate social responsibility programs
- Customer acquisition strategies
- Supplier development initiatives
- Community investment programs

Corporate grants are often less publicized than foundation grants, but they can be easier to access because there's typically less competition.

4. Industry Association Grants

Trade associations, professional organizations, and industry groups often provide grants to:

- Support innovation in their industries
- Help members grow their businesses
- Advance industry-wide goals
- Develop new markets or capabilities

These grants are often overlooked because people don't realize their industry associations offer funding programs.

THE RESEARCH STRATEGY

Effective grant research requires a systematic approach. Here's the strategy I teach my clients:

Step 1: Keyword Development

Create a comprehensive list of keywords related to your business impact:

- Your industry terms (obvious ones)
- Problem areas you address
- Demographics you serve
- Geographic areas you impact
- Social issues you help solve
- Economic outcomes you create

For example, a food truck business might use keywords like:

- Mobile food service
- Small business development
- Job creation
- Community development
- Minority-owned business
- Economic development
- Local food systems
- Entrepreneurship

Step 2: Database Searches

Use multiple databases to ensure comprehensive coverage:

Government Databases:

- Grants.gov (federal opportunities)
- State government websites
- Local economic development sites

Foundation Databases:

- Foundation Directory Online
- GrantSpace
- Foundation Center resources

General Grant Databases:

- GrantWatch
- Grant Station
- Government Grant Alert

Industry-Specific Resources:

- Trade association websites
- Professional organization grant lists
- Industry publication grant directories

Step 3: Geographic Targeting

Many grants prioritize or require applicants from specific geographic areas:

- Your city or county
- Your state or region

- Areas with specific economic designations (enterprise zones, opportunity zones, etc.)
- Rural or urban priority areas
- Areas affected by economic disruption

Research what special designations your location might have, as these can open additional funding opportunities.

Step 4: Demographic Considerations

If you qualify for any of these categories, they can significantly expand your grant opportunities:

- Women-owned business
- Minority-owned business
- Veteran-owned business
- Disabled-owned business
- Young entrepreneur (often under 35)
- Rural business owner
- Low-income entrepreneur

Many grants are specifically designated for these categories, and some give preference points even when not exclusively targeted.

THE SEARCH TOOLS AND RESOURCES

Free Resources:

Grants.gov: The official database of federal grant opportunities. Complex to navigate but comprehensive for government funding.

GrantSpace: Provides free access to Foundation Directory data and grant searching tools.

SCORE: Free mentoring organization that often maintains local grant databases.

Small Business Development Centers (SBDCs): Often have grant research assistance and local funding knowledge.

Local Libraries: Many have Foundation Directory access and librarians trained in grant research.

Paid Resources:

Foundation Directory Online: Most comprehensive foundation database, typically $200-500/year.

GrantWatch: User-friendly grant database with good search functionality, around $40/month.

Grant Station: Focuses on nonprofit and government grants, approximately $50/month.

Industry-Specific Resources:

Trade Association Websites: Often list member funding opportunities.

Professional Journals: Frequently publish grant opportunity announcements.

Industry Conferences: Networking can reveal funding sources not widely publicized.

THE OPPORTUNITY EVALUATION FRAMEWORK

Not every grant you find will be worth pursuing. Use this framework to evaluate opportunities:

Alignment Score (1-10):

- How well does this grant align with your business mission?
- Do you genuinely care about the funder's goals?
- Would you be proud to partner with this organization?

Qualification Score (1-10):

- Do you clearly meet the eligibility requirements?
- Do you have the capacity to complete the proposed project?
- Can you provide all required documentation?

Competition Assessment (1-10):

- How many other applicants are likely to apply?
- How well-positioned are you compared to typical applicants?
- Do you have any competitive advantages?

Resource Requirement (1-10):

- How much time will the application require?
- Do you have access to all necessary information?
- Can you meet the deadline comfortably?

Impact Potential (1-10):

- How much funding is available?

- Would winning this grant significantly impact your business?
- Could success lead to additional opportunities?

Focus your efforts on opportunities that score highest across these factors.

THE TIMING STRATEGY

Grant funders operate on different cycles:

Annual Cycles: Many foundations and government programs have once-yearly application periods. Missing the deadline means waiting a full year for the next opportunity.

Quarterly Cycles: Some funders accept applications four times per year, giving you more frequent opportunities.

Rolling Deadlines: A few funders accept applications continuously until their annual funding is exhausted.

Special Initiatives: Occasionally, funders launch special programs with unique timelines.

Emergency Funding: Some funders provide rapid response grants for crisis situations.

Create a calendar tracking application deadlines for grants you want to pursue. Start preparing applications well in advance of deadlines.

THE RELATIONSHIP BUILDING APPROACH

While grants are typically awarded based on merit, relationships can provide advantages:

Information Access: Connected applicants often learn about opportunities before they're widely publicized.

Application Guidance: Relationships can provide insights into what funders really want to see in applications.

Feedback Opportunities: Some funders will provide pre-application feedback to applicants they know.

Future Opportunities: Success with one grant can lead to introductions to other funders.

Program Intelligence: Relationships help you understand funder priorities and preferences.

Build relationships by:

- Attending funder events and workshops
- Following funders on social media
- Participating in programs they sponsor
- Volunteering for causes they support
- Connecting with previous grant recipients

THE DOCUMENTATION SYSTEM

Organize your grant research using a systematic approach:

Grant Opportunity Tracker:

- Funder name and contact information
- Grant program name and description
- Funding amount and duration
- Eligibility requirements
- Application deadline
- Required documents
- Your alignment and qualification scores

Application Calendar:

- All upcoming deadlines
- Preparation timeline for each application
- Required document gathering schedules
- Follow-up and notification dates

Funder Profiles:

- Mission and priorities
- Previous grant recipients
- Application preferences and requirements
- Contact relationships and interactions
- Success rate and feedback received

Results Tracking:

- Applications submitted
- Responses received
- Feedback and lessons learned

- Success rate analysis
- Future opportunity planning

THE COMMON RESEARCH MISTAKES

Mistake #1: Industry Tunnel Vision Searching only within your obvious industry category.

Solution: Think about all the impacts your business creates and search across multiple categories.

Mistake #2: Geographic Limitations Assuming you can only apply for local grants.

Solution: Many grants are open to applicants from multiple states or regions.

Mistake #3: Size Assumptions Believing you're too small or too new to qualify.

Solution: Many funders specifically target early-stage or small businesses.

Mistake #4: Deadline Panic Finding grants with deadlines that are too close to prepare quality applications.

Solution: Build a research routine that identifies opportunities months in advance.

Mistake #5: Information Overload Trying to apply for every grant you find instead of focusing on the best matches.

Solution: Use the evaluation framework to prioritize opportunities.

THE ONGOING RESEARCH HABIT

Grant research isn't a one-time activity—it should become an ongoing business habit:

Weekly Research: Spend 1-2 hours each week searching for new opportunities.

Monthly Review: Evaluate your grant calendar and application pipeline.

Quarterly Assessment: Analyze your success rate and adjust your strategy.

Annual Planning: Set grant funding goals and develop annual application strategies.

Relationship Maintenance: Stay connected with funders and previous contacts.

This consistent approach ensures you don't miss opportunities and helps you build momentum over time.

YOUR RESEARCH ACTION PLAN

Before moving to the next chapter, complete these tasks:

1. **Complete the Impact Mapping Exercise**: Identify all the ways your business creates value.
2. **Develop Your Keyword List**: Create comprehensive search terms based on your impact areas.

3. **Research Your Geographic Advantages**: Identify special designations or priority areas that apply to your location.

4. **Set Up Your Documentation System**: Create spreadsheets or databases to track opportunities and applications.

5. **Conduct Your First Search**: Spend 2-3 hours exploring different databases and identifying potential opportunities.

6. **Evaluate 5-10 Opportunities**: Use the evaluation framework to prioritize the most promising grants.

7. **Create Your Application Calendar**: Map out deadlines and preparation timelines for your top opportunities.

Remember: The goal isn't to find every possible grant—it's to find the grants that are the best match for your business and mission. Quality research leads to quality applications, which lead to funding success.

In the next chapter, we'll dive into writing grant applications that win. But first, you need to find the right opportunities to pursue. Take the time to do this research thoroughly—it's the foundation of everything that follows.

Your perfect grant funders are out there waiting to partner with you. You just need to know how to find them.

CHAPTER 12

THE PERFECT APPLICATION

"One of the biggest mistakes is not positioning their business or not talking about how they're going to use the funding. Most of the time, when people think about grants, they think about getting funding for hardship, but they don't position what will happen, what's the next step of their business when they get the funding that they're requesting."

This is the heart of why most grant applications fail. People focus on their problems instead of their solutions. They talk about what they need instead of what they'll create. They position themselves as charity cases instead of strategic partners.

Writing a winning grant application isn't about having perfect grammar or using fancy words. It's about clearly communicating why your business deserves investment and what that investment will achieve. It's about painting a picture so compelling that funders can't wait to be part of your success story.

In this chapter, I'm going to break down exactly how to write applications that get approved, using the same framework that has helped my clients secure millions in funding.

THE FUNDAMENTAL SHIFT IN THINKING

Before we dive into the mechanics of application writing, you need to understand the fundamental difference between applications that win and applications that lose.

Losing Applications Sound Like This:

- "Our business is struggling due to..."
- "We need funding to pay bills and stay afloat..."
- "Without this grant, we might have to close..."
- "Times are tough and we're behind on payments..."

Winning Applications Sound Like This:

- "We have an opportunity to expand our impact by..."
- "With additional funding, we can serve 50% more families while creating five new jobs..."
- "This investment will allow us to launch a program that addresses the critical need for..."
- "We're ready to scale our proven model to serve three additional communities..."

See the difference? Winners focus on opportunity, impact, and outcomes. Losers focus on problems, needs, and survival.

This isn't about being dishonest about your challenges. It's about leading with your vision instead of your problems.

THE ANATOMY OF A WINNING APPLICATION

Every successful grant application contains these essential elements, though they may be organized differently depending on the funder's requirements:

1. Executive Summary: The elevator pitch that determines whether reviewers keep reading **2. Problem Statement**: The issue your business addresses (not your business's problems) **3. Solution Description**: How your business solves the identified problem **4. Impact Plan**: What outcomes your funding will achieve **5. Implementation Strategy**: How you'll execute your plan **6. Budget and Justification**: Exactly how you'll use the money **7. Evaluation Methods**: How you'll measure and report success **8. Organizational Capacity**: Why you're qualified to succeed **9. Sustainability Plan**: How the impact will continue beyond the grant period

Let's break down each section in detail.

THE EXECUTIVE SUMMARY: YOUR MAKE-OR-BREAK MOMENT

The executive summary is typically the first thing reviewers read and often determines whether they'll carefully review the rest of your application. You have 200-300 words to capture their attention and make them want to fund your project.

What to Include:

- One compelling sentence about the problem you're solving
- A clear statement of your solution

- The specific funding amount you're requesting
- The key outcomes this funding will achieve
- Why you're the right organization to deliver these results

Executive Summary Example: "Working families in downtown Atlanta struggle to find quality, affordable childcare that accommodates their irregular work schedules, forcing many parents to choose between career advancement and their children's care. Little Stars Learning Center requests $25,000 to expand our successful extended-hours childcare program, enabling us to serve 30 additional children while creating five new jobs for early childhood educators in our community. This expansion will directly support working families, stimulate local economic development, and provide educational programming that prepares children for academic success. As the only childcare center in our area offering 6 AM to 9 PM coverage, we have a proven model ready for scaling and a waiting list of 50 families eager for our services."

What Makes This Work:

- Leads with a problem that matters to funders
- Positions the business as the solution
- Specific funding request
- Clear, measurable outcomes
- Evidence of demand and organizational capacity

THE PROBLEM STATEMENT: FOCUS ON COMMUNITY, NOT COMPANY

This is where many applications go wrong. Instead of describing the problems their business faces, winning applications describe problems in the community or industry that their business is positioned to solve.

Wrong Approach: "Our daycare is struggling because regulations changed and we're having trouble meeting the new requirements. We need funding to help us comply with state standards."

Right Approach: "Working parents in our community face a critical shortage of quality, affordable childcare, with over 200 families on waiting lists for the three existing centers in our area. This shortage forces parents to make difficult choices between career advancement and family responsibilities, ultimately limiting economic mobility for entire families."

Problem Statement Framework:

1. **Identify the Community Problem**: What issue exists in your area or industry?
2. **Quantify the Impact**: How many people are affected? What's the cost of inaction?
3. **Explain Current Gaps**: Why aren't existing solutions adequate?
4. **Connect to Funder Priorities**: How does this problem relate to what the funder cares about?

THE SOLUTION DESCRIPTION: POSITION YOUR BUSINESS AS THE ANSWER

Your solution section should clearly explain how your business addresses the problem you've identified, but more importantly, why your approach is uniquely effective.

Solution Framework:

1. **Direct Connection**: Clearly link your solution to the problem
2. **Unique Value**: What makes your approach different or better?
3. **Evidence of Effectiveness**: What proof do you have that your solution works?
4. **Scalability**: How can success be expanded or replicated?

Solution Example: "Little Stars Learning Center addresses this childcare shortage through our innovative extended-hours model, providing quality early childhood education from 6 AM to 9 PM to accommodate various work schedules. Our approach combines state-certified early childhood educators with a play-based learning curriculum that prepares children for kindergarten success. In our first year, 95% of our kindergarten-age graduates met or exceeded school readiness benchmarks, and parent surveys showed 89% reported increased job satisfaction due to reliable childcare. Our model is scalable and replicable, providing a blueprint for addressing similar childcare shortages in other communities."

THE IMPACT PLAN: PAINT THE PICTURE OF SUCCESS

This is where you get specific about what the grant funding will accomplish. Funders want to see measurable outcomes that align with their mission and priorities.

Types of Impact to Highlight:

- **Quantitative Outcomes**: Numbers of people served, jobs created, revenue generated
- **Qualitative Outcomes**: Quality improvements, capacity building, skill development
- **Economic Impact**: Local spending, tax revenue, business growth
- **Social Impact**: Community strengthening, problem-solving, quality of life improvements
- **Educational Impact**: Skills developed, knowledge transferred, capacity built

Impact Plan Example: "This $25,000 investment will enable Little Stars Learning Center to:

- Serve 30 additional children from working families (100% increase in capacity)
- Create 5 new full-time positions for early childhood educators
- Generate approximately $180,000 in annual parent savings on childcare costs
- Support 30 families in maintaining or advancing their careers
- Provide 150 hours of parent education programming annually
- Contribute $15,000 annually in local taxes and economic activity

- Serve as a model for childcare expansion in three neighboring communities"

The Key: Be specific, be realistic, and connect every outcome to something the funder cares about.

THE IMPLEMENTATION STRATEGY: PROVE YOU CAN DELIVER

Funders want to know that you have a realistic plan for achieving the outcomes you've promised. This section demonstrates your organizational competence and project management skills.

Implementation Elements:

- **Timeline**: When will key milestones be achieved?
- **Activities**: What specific steps will you take?
- **Resources**: What tools, staff, or materials will you need?
- **Partnerships**: Who will you work with to ensure success?
- **Risk Management**: What could go wrong and how will you address it?

Timeline Example: "Month 1-2: Facility renovation and licensing updates Month 3: Staff recruitment and training Month 4: Program launch with initial 15 children Month 6: Full capacity of 30 additional children Month 12: Program evaluation and replication planning"

THE BUDGET: EVERY DOLLAR HAS A PURPOSE

Your budget should be detailed, realistic, and directly connected to your implementation plan. Every line item should contribute to achieving your stated outcomes.

Budget Categories:

- **Personnel**: Salaries, benefits, training costs
- **Equipment**: Technology, furniture, supplies
- **Facilities**: Rent, utilities, renovation costs
- **Program Costs**: Materials, supplies, activities
- **Administrative**: Insurance, licensing, professional services
- **Evaluation**: Data collection, reporting, analysis

Budget Justification Example: "Staff Salaries ($18,000): Five part-time early childhood educators at $15/hour for 12 hours/week each, providing the additional coverage needed for extended hours programming.

Classroom Equipment ($4,000): Age-appropriate learning materials, safety equipment, and furniture required for licensing compliance and quality programming.

Training and Professional Development ($2,000): Initial 40-hour certification training for new staff plus ongoing professional development to maintain program quality.

Administrative Costs ($1,000): Licensing fees, insurance increases, and basic supplies needed to support expanded operations."

Budget Best Practices:

- Be specific about costs and how you determined them
- Show that you've done your research on market rates
- Include matching funds or in-kind contributions when possible
- Avoid round numbers that look like guesses
- Connect every expense to program outcomes

THE EVALUATION PLAN: PROVE YOUR IMPACT

Funders want to know how you'll measure success and report on the impact of their investment. A strong evaluation plan shows that you're committed to accountability and continuous improvement.

Evaluation Framework:

- **Output Measures**: What you'll produce (services delivered, people served)
- **Outcome Measures**: Changes that result from your work (skills gained, problems solved)
- **Impact Measures**: Long-term effects of your work (economic development, social change)

Data Collection Methods:

- **Quantitative Data**: Numbers, percentages, statistics
- **Qualitative Data**: Stories, testimonials, case studies
- **Baseline Data**: Where things stand before your intervention
- **Comparison Data**: How your results compare to alternatives

Evaluation Example: "Success will be measured through:

- Monthly enrollment tracking (target: 30 children enrolled within 8 months)
- Parent employment status surveys (target: 95% maintain or advance employment)
- Child development assessments (target: 90% meet kindergarten readiness benchmarks)
- Staff retention rates (target: 80% annual retention)
- Community economic impact analysis (target: $180,000 in parent savings annually)

Data will be collected monthly and reported quarterly, with a comprehensive annual report provided to all stakeholders."

THE ORGANIZATIONAL CAPACITY: WHY YOU'RE THE RIGHT CHOICE

This section proves that you have the skills, experience, and resources necessary to successfully implement your proposed project.

Elements to Include:

- **Leadership Background**: Relevant experience and qualifications
- **Organizational Track Record**: Previous successes and achievements
- **Financial Stability**: Evidence of sound financial management
- **Community Support**: Partnerships and endorsements

- **Unique Advantages**: What sets you apart from other potential applicants

Capacity Example: "Little Stars Learning Center is uniquely positioned to execute this expansion successfully:

Leadership: Director Jekwenta Primm brings 15 years of financial services experience and 3 years of childcare center management, combining business acumen with deep understanding of early childhood development.

Track Record: In our first year, we achieved 98% parent satisfaction ratings, zero safety incidents, and full enrollment within 6 months of opening.

Financial Management: We've maintained positive cash flow for 18 consecutive months and have established relationships with local banks for additional capital if needed.

Community Partnerships: We've developed formal partnerships with the Downtown Business Association, three local employers, and the Community College early childhood program for ongoing staff development.

Competitive Advantage: As the only childcare center in our area offering extended hours, we've built expertise in serving non-traditional work schedules that will be crucial for successful expansion."

THE SUSTAINABILITY PLAN: BEYOND THE GRANT

Funders want to know that their investment will create lasting impact, not just temporary solutions. Your sustainability plan should explain how the benefits of the grant will continue after the funding period ends.

Sustainability Strategies:

- **Revenue Generation**: How will ongoing costs be covered?
- **Capacity Building**: What systems or skills will be developed?
- **Partnership Development**: What relationships will support continued success?
- **Model Replication**: How can successful approaches be shared or scaled?

Sustainability Example: "Program sustainability will be ensured through:

- Increased tuition revenue from expanded enrollment covering ongoing operational costs
- Fee-for-service parent education programs generating additional revenue
- Partnership with local employers for corporate childcare contracts
- Training curriculum development for licensing to other childcare providers
- Annual fundraising events to support continued program enhancement"

THE COMMON APPLICATION MISTAKES

Mistake #1: Focusing on Your Problems Instead of Community Problems Wrong: "We need money because our business is struggling." Right: "Our community needs solutions to this critical problem."

Mistake #2: Vague or Unrealistic Outcomes Wrong: "This grant will help us grow our business." Right: "This grant will enable us to serve 50 additional families and create 8 new jobs."

Mistake #3: Poor Budget Justification Wrong: "Equipment: $5,000" Right: "Equipment: $5,000 for three age-appropriate learning stations at $1,200 each, plus safety materials and supplies."

Mistake #4: No Clear Connection Between Funding and Impact Wrong: "We need $25,000 for general operating expenses." Right: "This $25,000 will fund the specific resources needed to expand our program and serve 30 additional children."

Mistake #5: Weak Evidence of Organizational Capacity Wrong: "We're passionate about this work." Right: "Our track record includes 95% client satisfaction and 18 months of positive cash flow."

THE WRITING PROCESS

Step 1: Outline Before Writing Create a detailed outline that maps out each section before you start writing. This ensures logical flow and prevents important elements from being forgotten.

Step 2: Write Clearly and Concisely Use simple, direct language. Avoid jargon, acronyms, and complex sentences. Remember that reviewers may not be experts in your industry.

Step 3: Tell a Compelling Story Your application should have a narrative arc: problem → solution → impact → capacity → sustainability. Each section should build on the previous one.

Step 4: Use Data Strategically Include specific numbers and statistics to support your points, but don't overwhelm reviewers with unnecessary data.

Step 5: Edit Ruthlessly Every sentence should add value. Remove redundant information, unclear language, and anything that doesn't directly support your case for funding.

Step 6: Follow Guidelines Exactly Funders provide specific requirements for a reason. Follow page limits, formatting requirements, and submission procedures precisely.

THE REVIEW AND REFINEMENT PROCESS

Internal Review Checklist: ☐ Does the application clearly address the funder's priorities? ☐ Is the connection between funding and outcomes obvious? ☐ Are all budget items justified and necessary? ☐ Does the timeline seem realistic and achievable? ☐ Is the organizational capacity clearly demonstrated? ☐ Are all guidelines and requirements followed?

External Review Process: Have someone outside your organization review your application and answer these questions:

- What problem is this business solving?
- What will the grant funding accomplish?
- Why should this organization receive funding?
- What questions remain unanswered?

Final Polish:

- Proofread for grammar, spelling, and formatting
- Ensure all required documents are included

- Check that all deadline requirements are met
- Create backup copies of everything

YOUR APPLICATION ACTION PLAN

1. **Choose Your First Application**: Select one opportunity from your research to focus on initially.
2. **Gather Information**: Collect all required documents and information before you start writing.
3. **Create Your Outline**: Map out each section based on the funder's requirements.
4. **Write Your First Draft**: Focus on getting your ideas down without worrying about perfection.
5. **Review and Revise**: Use the frameworks in this chapter to strengthen each section.
6. **Get External Feedback**: Have someone else review your application for clarity and impact.
7. **Submit Early**: Don't wait until the last minute. Submit at least 24-48 hours before the deadline.

Remember: Your first application won't be perfect, and that's okay. The key is to submit strong applications consistently and learn from each experience. Every application you write makes the next one better.

In the next chapter, we'll explore what happens after you submit your application and how to maximize your chances of success throughout the entire grant process.

But for now, focus on crafting an application that clearly communicates why your business deserves investment and what that investment will achieve. The funding is out there—you just need to tell your story in a way that makes funders excited to be part of your success.

CHAPTER 13

BEYOND THE MONEY

"When you get that inventory, when you get that grant... you're building out a million dollar brand? Are you giving back to your community? Are you offering job opportunities? It's all about what you're going to do with the funding that separates you from the competition."

Most people think grant success ends when the check arrives. But that's actually when the real work begins. How you handle your grant funding—and the opportunities that come with it—determines whether you'll receive one grant or build a sustainable funding pipeline that supports your business for years to come.

In this chapter, I'm going to show you how to maximize the value of every grant you receive, build relationships that lead to additional funding, and create systems that turn grant success into long-term business growth.

Because here's the truth: the money is just the beginning. What you do beyond the money determines your ultimate success.

THE MINDSET SHIFT: FROM RECIPIENT TO PARTNER

The moment you receive a grant, your relationship with the funder changes. You're no longer an applicant hoping for approval—you're a partner working toward shared goals. This shift in mindset affects everything about how you handle the grant and the relationship.

As a Recipient, You Think:

- "I got the money, now I can relax"
- "I need to spend this quickly before they change their minds"
- "I hope they don't ask too many questions"
- "This relationship ends when the grant period is over"

As a Partner, You Think:

- "I need to deliver exceptional results to justify their investment"
- "I should use this funding strategically to maximize impact"
- "I want to keep them informed and engaged in our success"
- "This is the beginning of a long-term relationship"

Partners get invited back. Partners get referred to other funders. Partners get access to additional resources beyond just money.

Recipients get one check and disappear from the funder's radar.

THE IMPLEMENTATION EXCELLENCE FRAMEWORK

Once you receive grant funding, your primary job is to deliver on every promise you made in your application. But excellence goes beyond just meeting requirements—it's about exceeding expectations in ways that position you for future success.

Phase 1: Launch Excellence (First 30 Days)

Financial Setup:

- Create separate accounting codes for grant income and expenses
- Set up systems to track grant funds separately from other business money
- Establish reporting templates that match your application budget
- Schedule regular financial reviews to ensure you're on track

Communication Initiation:

- Send a professional thank-you letter acknowledging the grant
- Confirm your understanding of all grant requirements and deadlines
- Provide your contact information and communication preferences
- Schedule your first progress report date

Project Kickoff:

- Begin implementation according to your proposed timeline
- Document baseline data for all metrics you promised to track
- Take "before" photos if your project involves physical changes
- Create project files for organizing all grant-related documentation

Phase 2: Execution Excellence (Implementation Period)

Progress Tracking:

- Monitor your progress against the timeline in your application
- Track actual expenses against your approved budget
- Document all activities and outcomes as they occur
- Collect testimonials and success stories regularly

Proactive Communication:

- Send updates more frequently than required (monthly if they want quarterly)
- Share good news immediately—don't wait for formal reports
- Address challenges honestly and explain your solutions
- Include photos, testimonials, and concrete examples of impact

Relationship Building:

- Invite funders to visit your project or attend events
- Include them in relevant networking opportunities
- Share media coverage or recognition your project receives
- Ask for their input on challenges or opportunities

Phase 3: Completion Excellence (Final 30 Days)

Results Documentation:

- Compile comprehensive data on all outcomes achieved
- Create a compelling final report that tells the story of your success
- Include testimonials from beneficiaries and community partners
- Document lessons learned and best practices developed

Future Planning:

- Present your sustainability plan and how the impact will continue
- Identify opportunities for expansion or replication
- Propose potential future projects that align with the funder's mission
- Express interest in ongoing partnership

THE STRATEGIC SPENDING APPROACH

How you spend grant money sends a message about your business sophistication and commitment to impact. Strategic spending maximizes both your results and your credibility for future funding.

The 70-20-10 Rule

70% Direct Impact: Spend the majority of grant funds on activities that directly create the outcomes you promised.

20% Infrastructure: Invest in systems, tools, or capacity that will help you deliver better results and sustain impact.

10% Documentation and Promotion: Allocate funds for tracking results, creating reports, and sharing your success story.

Strategic Spending Examples

Instead of: Buying the cheapest equipment to save money *Do*: Invest in quality equipment that will last and perform better, then document how this choice improves outcomes

Instead of: Spending every dollar without tracking impact *Do*: Reserve funds for measuring and documenting results, which proves the value of the investment

Instead of: Keeping your success to yourself *Do*: Invest in professional photography, video testimonials, and marketing materials that showcase your impact

THE DOCUMENTATION AND STORYTELLING SYSTEM

Grants provide incredible content for building your business credibility and attracting additional opportunities. But you need systems to capture and leverage this content effectively.

Real-Time Documentation

Photo Documentation:

- Before/during/after photos of your project
- Action shots of activities and services
- Photos of people benefiting from your work (with permission)
- Images of equipment, facilities, or materials purchased

Video Content:

- Testimonials from people who benefit from your work
- Short videos showing your project in action
- Messages from staff or volunteers involved in the project
- Time-lapse documentation of physical changes or growth

Written Stories:

- Detailed case studies of individuals or families helped
- Staff reflections on the impact of the project
- Community responses and feedback
- Quantitative results and milestone achievements

Content Organization System

Create organized folders for:

- Grant-specific documentation
- General business impact stories
- Media-ready materials (high-resolution photos, edited videos)
- Testimonial collection
- Financial documentation and reports

This organized approach makes it easy to create compelling applications for future grants using evidence from your current success.

THE RELATIONSHIP LEVERAGE STRATEGY

Grant funders often have extensive networks that can benefit your business in ways beyond funding. Strategic relationship building can lead to:

Additional Funding Opportunities

- Introductions to other funders with similar missions
- Information about upcoming grant opportunities
- Invitations to funder collaboration events
- Access to capacity-building resources

Business Development Opportunities

- Connections to potential customers or clients
- Referrals to professional services (legal, accounting, marketing)
- Introductions to potential business partners
- Access to industry networks and associations

Professional Development Resources

- Invitations to training and educational events
- Mentorship opportunities with successful entrepreneurs
- Access to business development programs
- Speaking opportunities at conferences and events

Media and Publicity Support

- Features in funder newsletters and publications
- Social media promotion of your success
- Press release support for major milestones
- Award and recognition opportunities

THE REPORTING EXCELLENCE FRAMEWORK

Your grant reports are marketing documents disguised as compliance requirements. Excellence in reporting positions you for future funding and demonstrates your professionalism.

The Compelling Report Structure

Executive Summary: Lead with your most impressive results and impacts

Story Integration: Weave individual success stories throughout quantitative data

Visual Documentation: Include photos, charts, and graphics that illustrate your impact

Challenge Transparency: Address obstacles honestly and explain how you overcame them

Future Vision: Connect current success to future opportunities and potential

Gratitude Expression: Acknowledge the funder's role in enabling your success

Report Enhancement Strategies

Compare to Benchmarks: Show how your results compare to industry standards or previous years

Highlight Unexpected Benefits: Document positive outcomes you didn't anticipate in your original application

Include Third-Party Validation: Incorporate testimonials, media coverage, or independent evaluations

Demonstrate Learning: Explain how the grant experience improved your organization's capacity

Connect to Funder Mission: Explicitly link your results to the funder's goals and priorities

THE MEDIA AND PUBLICITY LEVERAGE

Grant success provides excellent content for business promotion, but many entrepreneurs fail to capitalize on these opportunities.

Press Release Strategy

Grant Award Announcement: When you receive the grant *Project Launch*: When you begin implementation *Milestone Achievements*: When you reach significant goals *Project Completion*: When you finish and can report final results

Social Media Amplification

Regular Updates: Share progress photos, testimonials, and milestone achievements *Behind-the-Scenes Content*: Show the work being done with grant funding *Beneficiary Spotlights*: Feature people who benefit from your grant-funded work *Funder Recognition*: Tag and thank your funders in social media posts

Content Marketing Opportunities

Blog Posts: Write about lessons learned and best practices developed *Case Studies*: Create detailed examples of impact for your website *Speaking Topics*: Use your grant success as credentials for speaking opportunities *Media Interviews*: Position yourself as an expert in your field based on your track record

THE EXPANSION AND REPLICATION STRATEGY

Successful grant projects often reveal opportunities for growth that you didn't anticipate in your original application.

Horizontal Expansion: Serving more people in the same way

- Increasing capacity at your current location
- Serving additional demographics with the same program
- Extending service hours or seasons

Vertical Expansion: Adding complementary services

- Providing additional services to existing clients
- Developing more comprehensive programming
- Creating pathways between different service levels

Geographic Expansion: Replicating success in new locations

- Opening additional locations
- Partnering with organizations in other communities
- Licensing your model to other providers

Systemic Impact: Changing how your industry operates

- Training other organizations to use your methods
- Advocating for policy changes based on your results
- Creating industry standards or best practices

THE SUSTAINABILITY TRANSITION

As your grant period ends, you need systems to maintain and build upon the impact you've created.

Revenue Diversification

Fee-for-Service Models: Can you charge for some services that were initially funded by grants?

Corporate Partnerships: Do your results interest corporate sponsors or partners?

Individual Fundraising: Can you build a donor base of people who support your mission?

Product Development: Can you create products or services that generate revenue while advancing your mission?

Operational Efficiency

Process Improvements: What systems did you develop that reduce costs or increase effectiveness?

Technology Integration: What tools make your work more efficient and scalable?

Staff Development: What skills did your team develop that increase capacity?

Partnership Leverage: What relationships reduce costs or increase impact?

THE FUTURE FUNDING PIPELINE

Grant success should position you for additional funding opportunities, not just celebrate a one-time achievement.

Funder Relationship Maintenance

Annual Updates: Keep successful funders informed about your continued progress *Program Invitations*: Invite them to relevant events and activities *Strategic Consultation*: Ask for their input on new initiatives and directions *Recognition Opportunities*: Acknowledge their support in awards, media coverage, and public events

Application Enhancement

Results Documentation: Use success data to strengthen future applications *Credibility Building*: Reference successful grants in new applications *Methodology Refinement*: Improve your approach based on what you learned *Network Expansion*: Use references and recommendations from successful grants

Strategic Planning Integration

Multi-Year Vision: Develop funding strategies that align with long-term business goals *Portfolio Approach*: Pursue grants of different sizes, types, and durations *Relationship Mapping*: Identify funders who might support different aspects of your work *Capacity Building*: Use grants to build capabilities that attract additional funding

THE COMMON POST-GRANT MISTAKES

Mistake #1: Disappearing After Receiving Funding Many recipients go silent after getting their check, missing opportunities to build relationships.

Solution: Maintain regular communication throughout the grant period and beyond.

Mistake #2: Spending Money Without Strategic Thinking Some recipients rush to spend funds without considering how purchases align with long-term goals.

Solution: Create spending plans that maximize both immediate impact and future capacity.

Mistake #3: Poor Documentation of Results Many recipients fail to adequately document their success, making it difficult to leverage for future opportunities.

Solution: Build documentation into your project plan from the beginning.

Mistake #4: Treating Reports as Chores Some recipients view reporting as administrative burden rather than marketing opportunity.

Solution: Approach reports as chances to showcase your impact and build relationships.

Mistake #5: Not Planning for Sustainability Many recipients don't think about how to maintain impact after grant funding ends.

Solution: Begin sustainability planning during the grant period, not after it ends.

YOUR BEYOND-THE-MONEY ACTION PLAN

1. **Create Your Documentation System**: Set up organized files for tracking impact, collecting testimonials, and storing media content.
2. **Develop Your Communication Calendar**: Plan regular updates to funders throughout your grant period.
3. **Build Your Reporting Templates**: Create professional formats for progress reports and final reports.
4. **Establish Your Media Strategy**: Plan how you'll promote your grant success and document your impact.
5. **Map Your Network Expansion**: Identify relationship-building opportunities that come with grant success.
6. **Plan Your Sustainability Strategy**: Begin thinking about how to maintain impact beyond the grant period.
7. **Design Your Future Funding Pipeline**: Create a strategy for leveraging current success into additional funding opportunities.

Remember: Grant funding is not just about the money you receive—it's about the doors that money opens, the relationships it creates, and the credibility it builds. Entrepreneurs who understand this principle build sustainable funding pipelines that support their businesses for years.

Those who just spend the money and move on miss the greatest opportunities that grants provide.

In the next chapter, we'll look at real success stories from entrepreneurs who have used these principles to secure substantial funding and build thriving businesses. You'll see exactly how the strategies we've discussed translate into real-world results.

But for now, start thinking beyond the money. Every grant is an investment in your future success—if you know how to leverage it properly.

CHAPTER 14

FROM FIRED TO FUNDED

"**K**athy came to me, didn't have a lot of background on applying for grants or getting that access to grant funding, and we kind of gave her the blueprint and showed her what to do. Within, I want to say, about 90 days, she got approved for her first grant, which was $15,000."

The numbers tell a story, but the real power is in the transformation. When I share that my clients have secured over $5 million in grant funding, people focus on the money. But what really matters is what that funding represents: dreams realized, businesses saved, families supported, and communities strengthened.

In this chapter, I want to take you inside the real stories of entrepreneurs who have used the strategies in this book to transform their businesses and their lives. These aren't celebrity success stories or people with special advantages. They're regular entrepreneurs who learned to think differently about funding and took action despite their fears and doubts.

Their journeys will show you what's possible when you combine the right strategies with persistent action.

KATHY'S STORY: THE RELUCTANT ENTREPRENEUR TURNED GRANT SUCCESS

Background: Kathy had been thinking about starting a business for years but kept talking herself out of it. She had no background in grant writing, limited business experience, and was convinced she couldn't compete with more experienced entrepreneurs.

The Challenge: Like many aspiring entrepreneurs, Kathy was trapped between her dreams and her fears. She wanted to start a business that would give her financial independence and allow her to make a difference in her community, but she didn't know how to access the capital needed to get started.

The Transformation: When Kathy first joined my program, she was hesitant and uncertain. "I don't know if I can really do this," she told me during our initial consultation. But something changed when she understood that grants weren't just for "other people" with special qualifications.

Within the first month, Kathy had:

- Registered her LLC and obtained her EIN
- Identified three potential grant opportunities
- Completed her first grant application
- Developed a clear business plan aligned with funder priorities

The First Success: Ninety days after joining the program, Kathy received her first grant approval: $15,000 for her for-profit business. The money was life-changing, but the confidence boost was even more valuable.

"I couldn't believe it," she said. "I kept thinking there must be some mistake. But then I realized—I really can do this."

The Expansion: Success built on success. Kathy didn't stop with her first grant. She used the credibility from her initial funding to start a nonprofit organization, which received a $25,000 grant just a few months later.

Total Funding: $40,000 in less than four months

The Real Success: Beyond the money, Kathy discovered something more valuable: her own capability. "I went from being afraid to even try to feeling confident that I can figure out how to fund whatever vision I have," she reflected. "That mindset shift changed everything about how I approach business and life."

Key Lessons from Kathy's Success:

- You don't need extensive experience to succeed with grants
- Success builds momentum that leads to more opportunities
- The confidence gained from grant success often exceeds the value of the funding
- Having a proven system makes the process much more manageable

EMMA'S STORY: FROM STRUGGLE TO SUSTAINABILITY

Background: Emma had been running her business for several years but was constantly struggling with cash flow. She was talented and hardworking, but traditional funding sources weren't accessible to her. She was considering closing her business when she discovered grants.

The Challenge: Emma's business was viable but undercapitalized. She needed funding for equipment, inventory, and working capital, but her credit wasn't strong enough for traditional loans, and she couldn't afford the equity dilution that investors would require.

The Learning Phase: Emma approached grants methodically. She spent time understanding different funder priorities and learning to position her business not just as a profit-making entity, but as a solution to problems funders cared about.

She discovered that her business:

- Created jobs in an economically disadvantaged area
- Provided services to underserved populations
- Supported environmental sustainability
- Contributed to local economic development

The Strategic Approach: Rather than applying for grants randomly, Emma developed a systematic approach:

- She researched funders whose missions aligned with her business impact
- She created detailed project proposals that connected funding to specific outcomes
- She built relationships with funders through networking and community involvement
- She leveraged each grant success to build credibility for the next application

The Results: Over 18 months, Emma secured funding from multiple sources:

- Economic development grants for job creation
- Environmental grants for sustainable business practices
- Community foundation grants for serving underserved populations
- Corporate grants for supplier diversity programs

Total Funding: Nearly $1 million from various sources

The Business Transformation: The funding allowed Emma to:

- Purchase equipment that increased efficiency and capacity
- Hire additional staff and provide competitive wages
- Expand into new markets and service areas
- Build cash reserves that provided stability and growth capital

The Personal Transformation: "Grants didn't just fund my business," Emma explained. "They taught me to think strategically about everything I do. Now I approach every business decision by asking, 'How does this create value for others?' That mindset has made me a better entrepreneur in every way."

Key Lessons from Emma's Success:

- Systematic approaches consistently outperform random efforts
- Multiple smaller grants can be more valuable than one large grant
- Grant success builds business credibility that attracts other opportunities
- Strategic thinking developed through grant applications improves overall business decisions

MEGAN'S STORY: THE GRANT PORTFOLIO APPROACH

Background: Megan understood from the beginning that grants could be a significant funding source for her entrepreneurial goals. Rather than treating grants as occasional opportunities, she approached them as a core business strategy.

The Vision: Megan didn't just want to start one business—she wanted to create a portfolio of organizations that addressed different aspects of the same community problem. She saw grants as the vehicle for building this vision systematically.

The Strategic Plan: Working with my framework, Megan developed a multi-organization strategy:

- Organization #1: A for-profit business that provided direct services
- Organization #2: A nonprofit that addressed the same issues through education and advocacy
- Organization #3: A social enterprise that created sustainable funding for both organizations

The Execution: Megan treated grant applications like a part-time job. She spent several hours each week researching opportunities, preparing applications, and maintaining relationships with funders.

Her approach included:

- Detailed tracking systems for all opportunities and deadlines

- Standardized templates that could be customized for different funders
- Regular communication with funders throughout grant periods
- Strategic timing of applications to create steady funding flow

The Portfolio Results:

- Organization #1: $800,000 in grants over two years
- Organization #2: $1.2 million in foundation and government grants
- Organization #3: $600,000 in corporate and community grants

Total Portfolio: $2.6 million across three organizations

The Lifestyle Design: Megan's grant portfolio allowed her to create the lifestyle she wanted:

- She works from home, setting her own schedule
- She's financially independent without traditional employment
- She's making significant impact in her community
- She's building sustainable organizations that will continue beyond her direct involvement

The Compound Effects: Success in one area created opportunities in others:

- Grant success led to speaking opportunities and consulting contracts
- Media coverage attracted additional funding and partnership opportunities
- Board positions and advisory roles expanded her network and influence

- Recognition and awards opened doors to resources and relationships

Key Lessons from Megan's Success:

- Treating grants as a systematic business strategy produces better results than occasional applications
- Multiple organizations can create synergies that benefit all entities
- Consistent effort compounds over time into extraordinary results
- Grant success can become a platform for broader entrepreneurial opportunities

THE COMMON SUCCESS PATTERNS

Analyzing these success stories and dozens of others reveals consistent patterns that distinguish highly successful grant recipients:

Pattern #1: Systems Thinking Successful grant recipients don't just apply for grants—they build systems for identifying opportunities, preparing applications, and managing relationships. They treat grant seeking as a business process that can be optimized and improved.

Pattern #2: Mission Alignment The most successful applicants genuinely care about the problems they're solving and the communities they're serving. This authenticity comes through in their applications and builds trust with funders.

Pattern #3: Long-Term Perspective Winners think beyond individual grants to build sustainable funding strategies. They use each grant to build capacity, credibility, and relationships that lead to additional opportunities.

Pattern #4: Professional Excellence Successful grant recipients treat every interaction with funders professionally. They meet deadlines, follow guidelines, communicate clearly, and deliver on their promises.

Pattern #5: Continuous Learning The best grant recipients constantly improve their approaches based on feedback and results. They learn from rejections, refine their strategies, and adapt to changing funder priorities.

THE TRANSFORMATION BEYOND MONEY

While the financial results are impressive, the real transformation these entrepreneurs experienced goes much deeper:

Confidence Building: Successfully competing for grants builds confidence that extends to every aspect of business and life. When you've convinced sophisticated funders to invest in your vision, you approach other challenges with greater self-assurance.

Strategic Thinking Development: The grant application process forces entrepreneurs to think strategically about their businesses, their markets, and their impact. This strategic thinking improves decision-making across all business activities.

Network Expansion: Grant success opens doors to networks and relationships that create opportunities beyond funding. Many of my clients have found mentors, partners, customers, and investors through their grant work.

Communication Skills Enhancement: Writing compelling grant applications improves entrepreneurs' ability to communicate their value proposition to any audience—customers, investors, partners, or media.

Community Connection: The grant process connects entrepreneurs more deeply with their communities and the problems they're solving. This connection often leads to additional business opportunities and personal fulfillment.

THE FAILURE STORIES AND LESSONS LEARNED

Not every grant application succeeds, and not every entrepreneur who learns these strategies immediately transforms their business. The failures teach us as much as the successes:

The Impatient Entrepreneur: Sarah applied for three grants, was rejected for all three, and gave up. She said, "This doesn't work for me." The lesson: Grant success requires persistence. Most successful applicants are rejected multiple times before winning funding.

The Unfocused Applicant: Mike applied for dozens of grants without carefully evaluating fit or quality. He spent enormous time on applications but had little success because he wasn't strategic about targeting. The lesson: Quality and focus matter more than quantity.

The Poor Executor: Lisa won a significant grant but failed to implement her project effectively. She didn't meet reporting requirements and damaged her relationship with the funder. The lesson: Winning the grant is just the beginning—execution determines long-term success.

The Lone Wolf: David refused to ask for help or feedback on his applications. He insisted on doing everything himself and was frustrated by consistent rejections. The lesson: Support and mentorship accelerate success.

THE SCALABILITY FACTOR

One of the most exciting aspects of grant success is how it scales beyond individual funding approvals:

Credibility Compounds: Each successful grant makes it easier to win additional grants. Funders want to invest in organizations with track records of success.

Networks Expand: Success with one funder often leads to introductions to other funders. The grant community is interconnected, and reputation travels quickly.

Expertise Develops: The more grants you win, the better you become at identifying opportunities, writing applications, and managing funder relationships.

Impact Multiplies: Successful grant recipients often become mentors and teachers for other entrepreneurs, multiplying the impact of their knowledge and experience.

Opportunities Diversify: Grant success often leads to speaking opportunities, consulting contracts, board positions, and other income streams.

THE COMMUNITY IMPACT

The success stories in this chapter represent more than individual business achievements—they demonstrate the community impact that results when entrepreneurs access appropriate funding:

Job Creation: Collectively, these entrepreneurs have created dozens of jobs in their communities, providing employment and economic opportunity for others.

Service Provision: Their businesses provide services and products that improve quality of life for thousands of people.

Economic Development: Their success contributes to local economic development and demonstrates what's possible for other entrepreneurs.

Inspiration and Mentorship: Their stories inspire other entrepreneurs and many have become mentors and teachers themselves.

Policy Influence: Their success helps convince funders and policymakers to continue supporting small business development and entrepreneurship.

YOUR SUCCESS STORY POTENTIAL

As you read these stories, consider what's possible for your own business and community:

What problems could you solve with appropriate funding? What impact could you create if you had access to grants? How would grant success change your business trajectory? What would

be possible for your family and community if you successfully accessed funding?

The entrepreneurs featured in this chapter started where you are now—with dreams, determination, and the willingness to learn new strategies. Their success isn't the result of special advantages or unique circumstances. It's the result of applying proven strategies consistently and persistently.

Your success story is waiting to be written. The funding is available. The strategies work. The only question is whether you're ready to take action.

In the next chapter, we'll create your personalized action plan for grant success, breaking down the journey into manageable steps you can begin implementing immediately.

But for now, let these stories sink in. Let them expand your vision of what's possible. Let them convince you that grant funding isn't just for other people—it's for entrepreneurs like you who are ready to solve problems and create value in their communities.

Your transformation from wherever you are now to where you want to be is not only possible—it's probable, if you're willing to do the work these successful entrepreneurs have done.

The question isn't whether you can succeed with grants. The question is: What will your success story look like?

CHAPTER 15

YOUR GRANT ACTION PLAN

"**Y**ou can be independent and still get help and support. One of the biggest mistakes I made on my journey is just not reaching out and not reaching out sooner."

We've covered a lot of ground in this book—from my journey of getting fired into freedom to the specific strategies that have helped my clients secure millions in grant funding. But knowledge without action is just expensive entertainment.

This chapter is where theory meets reality. It's your roadmap from wherever you are right now to submitting your first grant application and building a sustainable funding strategy for your business.

I'm going to break this down into a 30-day kickstart plan that will get you moving immediately, followed by a longer-term strategy for building grant success into your business operations.

Because here's the truth: The perfect time to start doesn't exist. The only time that matters is now.

THE 30-DAY GRANT KICKSTART PLAN

This plan assumes you can dedicate 5-10 hours per week to grant preparation. If you have more time available, you can accelerate the timeline. If you have less time, stretch it out but maintain momentum by working on it consistently.

WEEK 1: FOUNDATION BUILDING

Day 1-2: Business Structure Assessment

☐ **Legal Entity Status**: If you don't have an LLC or corporation, start the registration process immediately. Don't wait until everything else is perfect.

☐ **EIN Application**: Apply for your Employer Identification Number directly through the IRS website (free). This takes 10-15 minutes online.

☐ **Business Address**: Secure a professional business address if you don't have one. Research virtual office options or ask business connections about address sharing.

☐ **Documentation Organization**: Create physical and digital filing systems for all business documents.

Day 3-4: Digital Presence Audit

☐ **Website Review**: Assess your current website or create a basic one if needed. It doesn't need to be elaborate, but it should clearly explain what your business does.

☐ **Email Setup**: Get a professional email address that matches your domain name.

☐ **Social Media Audit**: Review your LinkedIn, Facebook, and other profiles to ensure they present a professional image.

☐ **Online Consistency**: Make sure your business name, description, and contact information are consistent across all platforms.

Day 5-7: Financial Foundation

☐ **Business Bank Account**: Open a dedicated business bank account if you don't have one.

☐ **Accounting System**: Set up basic bookkeeping using QuickBooks, FreshBooks, or organized spreadsheets.

☐ **Financial Projections**: Create realistic revenue and expense projections for the next 12-24 months.

☐ **Budget Planning**: Develop preliminary budgets for potential grant projects.

WEEK 2: IMPACT IDENTIFICATION AND POSITIONING

Day 8-10: Impact Mapping

☐ **Problem Identification**: List 3-5 significant problems in your community or industry that your business addresses.

☐ **Solution Articulation**: For each problem, clearly describe how your business provides solutions.

☐ **Impact Measurement**: Identify specific, measurable ways your business creates positive outcomes.

☐ **Beneficiary Analysis**: Define exactly who benefits from your work and how.

Day 11-12: Competitive Advantage Analysis

☐ **Unique Value Proposition**: Clearly articulate what makes your approach different or better than alternatives.

☐ **Qualification Assessment**: List your qualifications, experience, and capabilities that make you suited to solve these problems.

☐ **Success Documentation**: Gather evidence of any previous successes, testimonials, or positive outcomes.

☐ **Partnership Potential**: Identify potential partners who could strengthen your applications.

Day 13-14: Strategic Positioning Development

☐ **Mission Statement**: Create a clear, compelling mission statement that connects your business to larger social or economic goals.

☐ **Impact Categories**: Identify all the different types of impact your business creates (economic, social, educational, environmental, etc.).

☐ **Target Demographics**: Define the specific populations or geographic areas you serve.

☐ **Outcome Tracking**: Plan how you'll measure and document the results of grant funding.

WEEK 3: RESEARCH AND OPPORTUNITY IDENTIFICATION

Day 15-17: Grant Research

☐ **Keyword Development**: Create a comprehensive list of search terms related to your business impact.

☐ **Database Registration**: Sign up for free accounts on Grants.gov, GrantSpace, and relevant industry websites.

☐ **Initial Searches**: Spend 2-3 hours exploring different databases and identifying potential opportunities.

☐ **Opportunity Tracking**: Create a spreadsheet to track grants you discover, including deadlines, requirements, and fit scores.

Day 18-19: Funder Research

☐ **Funder Mission Analysis**: Research the missions and priorities of organizations that fund businesses like yours.

☐ **Previous Recipients**: Look up previous grant recipients to understand what funders value.

☐ **Application Requirements**: Note the specific requirements and preferences of your top 5-10 target funders.

☐ **Contact Information**: Gather contact information for relevant program officers and decision makers.

Day 20-21: Opportunity Evaluation

☐ **Fit Assessment**: Use the evaluation framework from Chapter 11 to score your top opportunities.

☐ **Timeline Planning**: Create a calendar showing application deadlines and preparation timelines.

☐ **Priority Setting**: Select your top 3-5 opportunities to focus on initially.

☐ **Resource Planning**: Assess what resources you'll need for each priority application.

WEEK 4: APPLICATION PREPARATION AND SUBMISSION

Day 22-24: Application Development

☐ **Template Creation**: Develop standard templates for common application sections (organizational capacity, impact measurement, etc.).

☐ **Supporting Documents**: Gather all necessary supporting documents (business licenses, financial statements, letters of support, etc.).

☐ **Budget Development**: Create detailed, realistic budgets for your priority grant opportunities.

☐ **Timeline Creation**: Develop specific implementation timelines for your proposed projects.

Day 25-27: Application Writing

☐ **First Draft**: Write complete first drafts of your top 1-2 applications using the frameworks from Chapter 12.

☐ **Review and Revision**: Review your drafts for clarity, completeness, and compliance with guidelines.

☐ **External Feedback**: Have someone outside your business review your applications and provide feedback.

☐ **Professional Polish**: Edit for grammar, formatting, and professional presentation.

Day 28-30: Submission and Follow-up

☐ **Final Review**: Complete final checks of all requirements and guidelines.

☐ **Submission**: Submit your first grant application at least 24-48 hours before the deadline.

☐ **Follow-up Planning**: Schedule follow-up communications and track submission confirmations.

☐ **Next Steps**: Begin preparing your next application while waiting for responses.

THE ONGOING GRANT STRATEGY

After your initial 30-day kickstart, grant success requires ongoing, systematic effort. Here's how to build grant activities into your regular business operations:

MONTHLY ACTIVITIES (2-4 Hours)

Opportunity Research:

- Search for new grant opportunities using your established keywords
- Review upcoming deadlines and application requirements
- Update your opportunity tracking spreadsheet
- Identify and research new potential funders

Relationship Building:

- Attend relevant networking events or webinars
- Follow target funders on social media and engage with their content
- Schedule coffee meetings with other grant recipients or industry contacts
- Participate in community activities that align with funder missions

System Maintenance:

- Update your supporting documents and templates
- Review and refresh your financial projections
- Document any new success stories or testimonials

- Organize and backup all grant-related files

QUARTERLY ACTIVITIES (4-8 Hours)

Strategy Review:

- Analyze your success rate and identify areas for improvement
- Review funder feedback and adjust your approach accordingly
- Update your business positioning based on new accomplishments
- Refine your target funder list based on results and insights

Application Development:

- Prepare and submit 1-3 grant applications per quarter
- Update your standard templates based on lessons learned
- Develop new project concepts that align with funder priorities
- Create or update supporting materials (photos, testimonials, case studies)

Relationship Deepening:

- Send updates to previous funders about your continued progress
- Invite funders to visit your project or attend relevant events
- Seek introductions to new funders through your existing network
- Participate in funder-sponsored events or training programs

ANNUAL ACTIVITIES (8-16 Hours)

Comprehensive Planning:

- Set annual grant funding goals and targets

- Develop a 12-month application calendar based on funder cycles
- Create or update your long-term business plan with grant integration
- Assess and improve your organizational capacity for managing grants

Major Relationship Initiatives:

- Plan and execute a funder appreciation event or update
- Seek board positions or volunteer opportunities with relevant organizations
- Develop strategic partnerships that strengthen your grant applications
- Create or participate in collaborative grant applications

System Overhaul:

- Conduct comprehensive review of all grant processes and systems
- Update all templates, documents, and supporting materials
- Analyze ROI of different types of grants and adjust strategy accordingly
- Plan and implement improvements to your impact measurement systems

THE ACCOUNTABILITY FRAMEWORK

Grant success requires consistent action over time. Here's how to maintain momentum and accountability:

WEEKLY CHECK-INS

Every Monday, spend 15 minutes reviewing:

- What grant activities did I complete last week?
- What grant activities do I need to complete this week?
- What obstacles or challenges do I need to address?
- What support or resources do I need to be successful?

MONTHLY ASSESSMENTS

At the end of each month, evaluate:

- How many grant opportunities did I research?
- How many applications did I submit?
- What feedback or responses did I receive?
- What did I learn that will improve future applications?
- Am I on track to meet my quarterly goals?

QUARTERLY REVIEWS

Every three months, conduct a comprehensive review:

- What was my success rate for the quarter?
- Which strategies are working best?
- What changes should I make to my approach?
- How can I improve my efficiency and effectiveness?
- What new opportunities or relationships should I pursue?

THE SUPPORT SYSTEM STRATEGY

Remember my lesson about independence versus isolation. Grant success is accelerated when you have the right support system in place.

PROFESSIONAL SUPPORT

Mentorship: Identify successful entrepreneurs or grant recipients who can provide guidance and advice.

Professional Services: Build relationships with attorneys, accountants, and other professionals who understand grant compliance and business development.

Peer Networks: Connect with other entrepreneurs who are pursuing grants or have grant experience.

Industry Associations: Join relevant trade associations and professional organizations that may offer grant resources or networking opportunities.

PERSONAL SUPPORT

Family Understanding: Help your family understand your grant strategy and how they can support your efforts.

Accountability Partners: Find someone who will check in on your progress and help you stay committed to your goals.

Cheerleaders: Identify people who believe in your vision and can provide encouragement during challenging periods.

Honest Feedback: Develop relationships with people who will give you constructive criticism to help improve your applications.

THE OBSTACLE ANTICIPATION PLAN

Every grant journey includes obstacles and setbacks. Here's how to prepare for and overcome common challenges:

CHALLENGE: REJECTION AND DISCOURAGEMENT

Preparation: Expect rejections and view them as learning opportunities rather than personal failures.

Response Strategy:

- Request feedback from funders when possible
- Analyze rejections to identify improvement opportunities
- Maintain perspective by remembering that successful grant recipients are rejected more often than they're approved
- Use rejections as motivation to improve your approach

CHALLENGE: TIME MANAGEMENT

Preparation: Build grant activities into your regular schedule rather than treating them as "extra" work.

Response Strategy:

- Block specific time each week for grant activities

- Batch similar activities (research, writing, follow-up) to improve efficiency
- Use templates and systems to reduce repetitive work
- Delegate or outsource other business activities to create time for grant work

CHALLENGE: INFORMATION OVERLOAD

Preparation: Focus on quality over quantity in your research and applications.

Response Strategy:

- Use the evaluation framework to prioritize opportunities
- Limit yourself to researching a specific number of grants per session
- Create clear criteria for which opportunities deserve your time
- Remember that pursuing fewer opportunities well is better than pursuing many opportunities poorly

CHALLENGE: IMPOSTER SYNDROME

Preparation: Document your qualifications, successes, and impact to remind yourself of your value.

Response Strategy:

- Keep a "success file" of testimonials, achievements, and positive feedback

- Remember that funders want to find qualified recipients— they're not trying to exclude you
- Focus on the problems you solve rather than your personal worthiness
- Seek support from mentors or peers who can provide perspective

THE SUCCESS MEASUREMENT SYSTEM

Track your progress using both quantitative and qualitative measures:

QUANTITATIVE METRICS

Activity Measures:

- Number of grant opportunities researched per month
- Number of applications submitted per quarter
- Number of funders contacted or engaged
- Hours invested in grant activities

Outcome Measures:

- Grant approval rate (applications approved ÷ applications submitted)
- Average funding amount per approved grant
- Total funding secured per year
- Time from application to decision

Efficiency Measures:

- Cost per dollar raised (time and resources invested ÷ funding secured)
- Application preparation time per grant
- Success rate by funder type or grant size
- ROI of different grant strategies

QUALITATIVE MEASURES

Relationship Development:

- Quality of funder relationships and communication
- Network expansion through grant activities
- Partnership opportunities created
- Recognition or reputation enhancement

Skill Development:

- Improvement in application quality over time
- Increased confidence in grant processes
- Enhanced business planning and strategic thinking capabilities
- Better understanding of funder perspectives and priorities

Business Impact:

- How grant funding advanced business goals
- Capacity building enabled by grant success
- Community impact created through grant activities
- Long-term sustainability improvements

YOUR PERSONAL ACTION COMMITMENT

Before closing this chapter, I want you to make specific commitments that will ensure you actually implement what you've learned:

IMMEDIATE COMMITMENTS (Next 7 Days)

I commit to completing these actions within one week:

☐ Register my business as a legal entity or verify my current registration
☐ Apply for my EIN or confirm I have the correct documentation ☐ Set up a dedicated business bank account or verify my current account setup
☐ Create a basic website or improve my existing website ☐ Complete the impact mapping exercise and identify 3-5 problems my business solves

SHORT-TERM COMMITMENTS (Next 30 Days)

I commit to completing the full 30-day kickstart plan, including:

☐ Building my complete business foundation ☐ Identifying and researching grant opportunities ☐ Preparing and submitting my first grant application ☐ Creating systems for ongoing grant activities

LONG-TERM COMMITMENTS (Next 12 Months)

I commit to building grant success into my business strategy by:

☐ Submitting a minimum of _____ grant applications over the next year ☐ Implementing the monthly, quarterly, and annual activities

outlined in this plan ☐ Building relationships with at least _____
funders or grant-related contacts ☐ Securing $_____ in grant funding
to support my business goals

ACCOUNTABILITY COMMITMENTS

I commit to creating accountability by:

☐ Sharing my grant goals with _____ (accountability partner name) ☐
Scheduling regular check-ins to review my progress ☐ Joining or creating a peer group of entrepreneurs pursuing grants ☐ Seeking mentorship
from someone who has succeeded with grants

THE REALITY CHECK

Let me be completely honest with you: Following this action plan won't
guarantee that you'll win every grant you apply for. Grant success requires
persistence, continuous learning, and the ability to handle rejection.

But I can guarantee this: If you follow this plan consistently, you will:

- Position yourself to compete effectively for grant funding
- Develop skills that improve all aspects of your business
- Build relationships that create opportunities beyond grants
- Create systems that support long-term business success
- Gain confidence in your ability to secure resources for your vision

Most importantly, you'll join the community of entrepreneurs who refuse
to let funding limitations prevent them from pursuing their dreams.

THE FINAL CHALLENGE

Everything you need to succeed with grants is in this book. You have the strategies, the frameworks, the examples, and now the action plan.

The only question remaining is: Will you take action?

I've shown you the path from fired to funded, from struggling to succeeding, from dreams to reality. But I can't walk the path for you.

Your transformation begins with the first step. Your success story starts with the first application. Your freedom begins with the first grant.

What are you waiting for?

In the epilogue, I'll share my final thoughts on the future of funding and the legacy you can create through grants. But for now, close this book and open your laptop.

Your grant journey starts today.

Action Step Right Now: Before you do anything else, go to your computer and complete one task from Day 1 of the 30-day plan. Don't wait for Monday. Don't wait for next month. Don't wait for the perfect time.

Start now.

Your future funded self is waiting.

THE FUTURE OF FUNDING

"I truly want to be the #1 source for everything grants—the go-to resource when it comes to getting education for funding, knocking down these doors of these corporations and telling them that we deserve money and capital, not because we're minorities, not because we're women, but because we have amazing companies that are structured the correct way and are providing resources and opportunities to our communities."

As I write these final words, I'm sitting in the home office that represents everything my journey has been about. On the walls are photos from workshops I've hosted, thank-you notes from clients who've secured funding, and awards recognizing the impact we've created together. But what moves me most is the picture of my daughter at her latest school event—an event I was able to attend because I built a business that gives me freedom to be present for what matters most.

This epilogue isn't just about grants or funding strategies. It's about the future I envision for entrepreneurs like you—a future where access to capital isn't determined by who you know or where you come from, but by the value you create and the problems you solve.

THE REVOLUTION WE'RE BUILDING

When I got fired from Wells Fargo, I couldn't have imagined that this painful experience would become the catalyst for a movement. But that's exactly what's happening. Every entrepreneur who learns to access grants is part of a quiet revolution that's changing how business funding works in America.

For too long, the funding landscape has been dominated by systems that favor the already privileged. Traditional bank loans require perfect credit and substantial collateral. Venture capital flows primarily to tech companies founded by people who look like the investors. Angel investors typically fund people in their networks, which often exclude women and minorities.

Grants represent something different: funding based on value creation rather than privilege protection.

When Kathy secured $40,000 in her first few months without any special connections, she proved that merit matters more than networks. When Emma built a nearly million-dollar funding portfolio through strategic thinking rather than inherited advantage, she demonstrated that intelligence and persistence can overcome systemic barriers. When Megan created a $2.6 million enterprise by treating grants as a systematic business strategy, she showed what's possible when entrepreneurs understand how funding really works.

These aren't isolated success stories. They're examples of what becomes possible when we democratize access to funding information and education.

THE MINDSET TRANSFORMATION

The real revolution isn't just about money—it's about mindset.

Traditional funding teaches entrepreneurs to position themselves as supplicants: "Please give us money because we need it." Grant funding teaches entrepreneurs to position themselves as partners: "Invest in us because we create value."

This shift from scarcity to abundance thinking affects every aspect of how entrepreneurs approach their businesses:

From "I need funding to survive" to "I deserve investment to thrive" From "I hope someone will take a chance on me" to "I'm offering funders an opportunity to achieve their goals" From "Funding is scarce and competitive" to "Funding is abundant for value creators" From "I have to do everything alone" to "Success requires strategic partnerships"

When entrepreneurs make this mindset shift, they don't just become better at winning grants—they become better at everything. They approach customers with more confidence, negotiate partnerships from positions of strength, and build businesses that create value rather than just extracting profit.

THE RIPPLE EFFECTS

Every entrepreneur who successfully accesses grants creates ripple effects that extend far beyond their individual business:

Job Creation: Grant-funded businesses create employment opportunities in their communities, often providing good-paying jobs to people who need them most.

Service Provision: These businesses provide products and services that improve quality of life, fill market gaps, and address community needs.

Economic Development: Successful entrepreneurs contribute to local tax bases, support other businesses through purchasing, and attract additional investment to their areas.

Inspiration and Mentorship: Their success stories inspire others to pursue entrepreneurship and many become mentors who help the next generation.

Cultural Change: They change perceptions about who can be successful in business and what types of ventures deserve support.

Policy Influence: Their success provides evidence that supports continued funding for small business development and entrepreneurship programs.

When we multiply these effects across thousands of grant recipients, we're talking about substantial economic and social impact. We're not just changing individual lives—we're strengthening entire communities.

THE DIGITAL ACCELERATION

Technology is making grant access more democratic than ever before. When I started my grant journey, finding opportunities required connections and insider knowledge. Today, databases and search tools make it possible for anyone to discover funding sources.

But technology alone isn't enough. Information without education is just data. That's why the work I do—and the work this book represents—is so crucial. We're not just providing information; we're providing the context, strategy, and support that turn information into results.

The future of funding education will likely include:

AI-Powered Matching: Technology that can match entrepreneurs with the most relevant funding opportunities based on their business characteristics and goals.

Virtual Reality Training: Immersive experiences that allow entrepreneurs to practice grant applications and funder interactions in realistic simulations.

Blockchain Verification: Systems that make it easier for funders to verify applicant credentials and track funding outcomes.

Global Collaboration: Platforms that connect entrepreneurs with funders and partners across geographic boundaries.

But the human element will remain essential. Successful grant applications require authentic storytelling, genuine relationship building, and strategic thinking that no algorithm can replace.

THE EDUCATION IMPERATIVE

One of the most important aspects of the grant revolution is its educational component. Learning to write grants teaches entrepreneurs skills that serve them throughout their business journeys:

Strategic Thinking: Grant applications force entrepreneurs to think systematically about their businesses, markets, and impact.

Communication Excellence: Writing compelling grant applications improves entrepreneurs' ability to communicate value to any audience.

Financial Planning: Grant budgets require detailed financial thinking that improves overall business management.

Impact Measurement: Grant reporting requirements teach entrepreneurs to track and analyze their results.

Relationship Building: Grant success requires developing and maintaining professional relationships with diverse stakeholders.

Persistence and Resilience: The grant process teaches entrepreneurs to handle rejection and continue pursuing their goals despite setbacks.

These skills compound over time, creating entrepreneurs who are more sophisticated, more strategic, and more successful in all aspects of their businesses.

THE GENERATIONAL WEALTH OPPORTUNITY

Perhaps the most exciting aspect of the grant revolution is its potential to create generational wealth in communities that have historically been excluded from traditional funding sources.

When entrepreneurs use grants to build successful businesses, they don't just improve their own financial situations—they create assets that can be passed down to their children. They model entrepreneurship as a viable path to prosperity. They build networks and knowledge that benefit their entire families.

My daughter is growing up watching me build businesses, access funding, and create opportunities. She's learning that entrepreneurship is possible, that funding is accessible, and that building something of value is within her reach. Those lessons will serve her throughout her life, regardless of what career path she chooses.

This is how we break cycles of financial dependence and build cycles of wealth creation. Not through charity or handouts, but through education, opportunity, and the confidence that comes from proven success.

THE CORPORATE RESPONSIBILITY EVOLUTION

The business world is evolving toward greater recognition of corporate social responsibility and stakeholder capitalism. This evolution creates more opportunities for grant funding as corporations realize that supporting small businesses and community development isn't just good PR—it's good business.

Forward-thinking corporations are discovering that grant programs can:

Build Customer Loyalty: Supporting businesses that serve their customer communities creates emotional connections and brand loyalty.

Develop Supply Chains: Investing in small business development creates potential suppliers and partners.

Strengthen Communities: Healthy communities provide better markets for corporate products and services.

Attract Talent: Employees want to work for companies that make positive social impact.

Generate Innovation: Small businesses often develop innovative solutions that larger corporations can adopt or acquire.

This trend means more grant opportunities for entrepreneurs who understand how to position their businesses as solutions to problems corporations care about.

THE POLICY IMPLICATIONS

The success of grant-funded entrepreneurs provides evidence for policy makers about the effectiveness of small business support programs. When politicians see that relatively small investments in grants can create jobs, generate tax revenue, and solve community problems, they're more likely to support continued funding.

This creates a positive feedback loop: successful grant recipients justify continued program funding, which creates more opportunities for future entrepreneurs.

The entrepreneurs using grants effectively today are creating the evidence base that will support expanded funding opportunities for tomorrow's business owners.

THE PERSONAL TRANSFORMATION LEGACY

Beyond the business outcomes and community impact, the grant revolution creates personal transformation that extends into every area of life.

Learning to successfully compete for grants builds confidence that affects how people approach all challenges. Understanding that you can convince sophisticated funders to invest in your vision changes how you see yourself and your capabilities.

This confidence is contagious. When people see you transform your circumstances through strategic action, they begin to believe that transformation is possible for them too.

When my father asked why I didn't reach out for help sooner, he was really asking about something deeper: why I didn't believe I was worthy of support. The grant process taught me that seeking support isn't a sign of weakness—it's evidence of strategic thinking.

That lesson affects how I parent, how I build relationships, and how I approach every challenge. It's a legacy I'm passing to my daughter and to every entrepreneur I work with.

THE VISION FORWARD

I envision a future where:

Every entrepreneur knows that grants exist and understands how to access them.

Funding decisions are based on value creation rather than personal connections.

Small businesses have the resources they need to solve problems and serve communities.

Entrepreneurship is recognized as a viable path to prosperity for people from all backgrounds.

Communities are strengthened by locally-owned businesses that create jobs and provide services.

Young people grow up believing that building businesses and accessing capital is within their reach.

This vision is achievable, but it requires continued education, advocacy, and action from people who understand the power of democratic access to funding.

THE NEXT GENERATION

As I look toward the future, I'm particularly excited about the entrepreneurs who are just beginning their journeys. They're growing up in a world where information is more accessible, networks are more global, and funding sources are more diverse than ever before.

They're also growing up with different expectations about what work should provide. They want careers that offer meaning, flexibility, and the opportunity to make a positive impact. Entrepreneurship—particularly when supported by strategic funding—can provide all of these things.

The next generation of entrepreneurs will likely be more sophisticated about funding, more strategic about building businesses, and more focused on creating sustainable impact. They'll build on the foundation we're creating today and take it to levels we can't yet imagine.

THE RESPONSIBILITY TO SHARE

If you successfully use the strategies in this book to access grant funding, you'll join a special community of entrepreneurs who understand something that most people don't: that funding is accessible to those who know how to seek it effectively.

With that knowledge comes responsibility. You have an obligation to share what you learn, to mentor others who are starting their journeys, and to be an example of what's possible.

This doesn't mean you have to become a grant consultant or write a book. It means being generous with information, encouragement, and introductions when opportunities arise. It means remembering that your success was built partly on the foundation created by others who shared their knowledge with you.

The grant revolution spreads through networks of entrepreneurs who believe in each other's success and are willing to invest in each other's growth.

THE CALL TO ACTION

As you close this book and begin implementing its strategies, remember that you're not just pursuing funding for your business—you're participating in a movement that's democratizing access to capital and creating opportunities for the next generation.

Your success matters beyond your bank account. It matters to your family, your community, and to other entrepreneurs who are watching to see what's possible.

Don't underestimate the power of your individual action. Every grant you apply for, every relationship you build, and every success you achieve contributes to a larger transformation in how business funding works.

The future of funding isn't just about new technologies or policy changes—it's about entrepreneurs like you who refuse to accept that traditional barriers should limit their potential.

THE FINAL PROMISE

I promise you this: if you consistently apply the strategies in this book, you will access funding that transforms your business and your life. You will build skills that serve you in every entrepreneurial endeavor. You will create value that benefits your community and your family.

But more than that, you will prove to yourself that you have the capability to achieve goals that once seemed impossible. You will discover resources and opportunities that you didn't know existed. You will build relationships that enrich your life beyond business.

You will go from wherever you are now to wherever you want to be. Not because funding is magic, but because the process of successfully accessing funding requires you to develop the mindset, skills, and relationships that create success in every area of life.

The entrepreneurs featured in this book started where you are now. They faced the same doubts, the same challenges, and the same uncertainty about whether grants were really accessible to people like them.

They succeeded not because they were special, but because they were willing to learn new strategies and take consistent action despite their fears.

Their success proved what I've always believed: that the resources exist to support every entrepreneur who is willing to create value and serve others.

Now it's your turn.

Your journey from fired to funded starts with the next step you take. Your transformation from where you are to where you want to be begins with the first application you submit.

The funding is out there. The opportunities are waiting. The future is ready for what you're going to build.

What are you waiting for?

In memory of every entrepreneur who gave up on their dreams because they didn't know that funding was accessible to them.

In honor of every entrepreneur who is building something that matters, regardless of the obstacles they face.

In anticipation of every entrepreneur who will use this book to transform their business and their life.

The revolution continues with you.

—Jekwenta "Coach K" Primm
The Grant Expert™

www.ingramcontent.com/pod-product-compliance
Lightning Source LLC
Chambersburg PA
CBHW060128130626
46556CB00006B/2274